Ketogenic Diet Guide

with 101 Keto Recipes

14 Days Fat Burning

for Perfect Weight Loss

Tanya Baker

Legal & Disclaimer

The information contained in this book and its contents is not designed to replace or take the place of any form of medical or professional advice; and is not meant to replace the need for independent medical, financial, legal or other professional advice or services, as may be required. The content and information in this book has been provided for educational and entertainment purposes only.

The content and information contained in this book has been compiled from sources deemed reliable, and it is accurate to the best of the Author's knowledge, information and belief. However, the Author cannot guarantee its accuracy and validity and cannot be held liable for any errors and/or omissions. Further, changes are periodically made to this book as and when needed. Where appropriate and/or necessary, you must consult a professional (including but not limited to your doctor, attorney, financial advisor or such other professional advisor) before using any of the suggested remedies, techniques, or information in this book.

Upon using the contents and information contained in this book, you agree to hold harmless the Author from and against any damages, costs, and expenses, including any legal fees potentially resulting from the application of any of the information provided by this book. This disclaimer applies to any loss, damages or injury caused by the use and application, whether directly or indirectly, of any advice or information presented, whether for breach of contract, tort, negligence, personal injury, criminal intent, or under any other cause of action.

You agree that by continuing to read this book, where appropriate and/or necessary, you shall consult a professional (including but not limited to your doctor, attorney, or financial advisor or such other advisor as needed) before using any of the suggested remedies, techniques, or information in this book.

TABLE OF CONTENT

INTRODUCTION

Previously like popular Hollywood celebrities I accompanied alkaline, raw and smoothie weight loss plan's for reducing weight, balances the pH, anti-aging and to keep away from a few fitness problems like arthritis and cancers, but how an awful lot ever I do physical activities and follow the eating regimen I faced some issues and felt involved in decreasing stubborn stomach fats, then after detail research and seeing effects I followed new diet called KETOGENIC DIET, you might heard but however you didn't attempt it, Actually it's a modified Atkins food regimen.

At first, congratulations for deciding on Ketogenic Diet Recipes for Weight Loss with less carbs, these recipes lets you lose weight, gain fitness, energy, and vitality. Coming to data, there are many extraordinary kinds of advantages of the ketogenic weight loss program, but due to lack of expertise, people are lacking safe way to shed pounds and doing away with fat from the body to keep healthful lengthy lifestyles.

Many have tried to do the weight reduction regimes of keeping exceptional diets, including on the weight reduction tablets and shakes, then religiously the use of sure workout machines offered at some point of the late night surfing of the TV or the net, only to have it either fail inside the pursuit of weight loss or to gain some nominal fulfillment however then gain lower back all of the weight and extra whilst the weight-reduction plan will become too hard to undergo. Does this all sound acquainted?

This eBook will draw up the benefits of the ketogenic eating regimen for you, speak approximately how and why the ketogenic diet works and most importantly, come up with based easy to follow steps on getting started and preserving the ketogenic eating regimen for the blessings of weight loss and better health. There are some ways to make scrumptious and nutritious keto recipes than just adding bunches of ingredients willy-nilly. So, to avoid this, within the following chapters will provide an explanation for each and every step of training method which includes fitness blessings and dietary statistics.

Additionally, you will learn various kind types of useful hints and recommendations to make certain your weight reduction plan habit develops as quick and easily as feasible, such as a way to completely commit to the eating regimen. After that you will discover top 136 ketogenic recipes for speedy weight loss in 28 days with less carbs which include breakfast, lunch, dinner, snack, dessert and smoothie's recipes regardless in case you are interested in preparing them to lose weight and increase health with boosted energy. This recipe guarantees that you'll lose weight in much less time period without losing your fitness.

I definitely have confidence that this eBook will give you the self assurance and expertise to start embarking for your own ketogenic journey. The key to begin a new diet successfully and effectively is doing everything within your power and dedication to lessen your weight via following a ketogenic diet, Successful pattern formations are a reminder, habitual and praise yourself with extra keto dessert and reminded yourself about incredible advantages.

CHAPTER 1:
Ketogenic Diet And Why It Works

The ketogenic diet is a excessive-fat, low carbohydrate food regimen that has comparable characteristics like Atkins and low-carb diets. Basically, required total energy for the body accumulated from glucose or sugar, however while you reduce carbohydrate consumption, the body starts to burn stored fats in the body for energy. These makes your body to go metabolic state called as "Ketosis", because of this, hormone insulin could be reduced and release of fatty acids might be extra and when fatty acids are transferred to the liver for digestion than it'll be oxidized and changed to ketones and supplies required energy to the mind. Typically, brain cells required glucose as a gasoline, however while the body goes to the hunger state, mind gets 25% to 60% of strength from ketones due to low carbohydrate consumption and turns protein to glucose for last energy, the process of converting protein too little glucose in the mind is referred to as gluconeogenesis. When you start burning fat cells, mechanically body starts off-evolved dropping weight immediately, and you'll feel and appearance higher from the inner out. The primary purpose of a ketogenic weight loss program is to convert your body into a fats-burning device. Such a weight loss program is loaded with benefits and is particularly endorsed through nutritional experts for the subsequent quit outcomes:

- **Weight Reduction**: The ketogenic food regimen facilitates to lessen weight faster than different meals's as it lowers the insulin level and begins burning stored fats
- **Blood Sugar**: Blood sugar ranges will be improved because it reduces glucose and glycated hemoglobin in whole body. Researchers identified that weight loss plan will result in decrease the blood pressure in overweight or obese individuals and allows to reduce strokes and heart diseases
- **Cholesterol**: Keto will helps to reduce the bad ldl cholesterol and increases required good cholesterol, that's essentially important for the body
- **Acne**: Recent human research have shown a drastic drop in pimples lesions and skin irritation over 10-12 weeks
- **Energy**: This makes and additionally offers your body more dependable required energy, which maintains your body more energizes in the course of an afternoon
- This weight loss program is used to treat and opposite Alzheimer's signs and symptoms ad even kills the most cancers cells
- Recently, medical doctors commenced recommending a ketogenic eating regimen for neurologic disorders along with autism and brain tumors
- Due to greater fat and protein consumption, it evidently suppresses the sugar and hunger cravings for a long time

Overall, the ketogenic regimen is to force your body into this metabolic level. We don't reap this through starvation of calories, however we acquire via starvation of carbohydrates. Our bodies is relatively adaptive, so in case you overload it with fatty items and avoid carbs, it's going to start to burn ketones as the primary energy for body.

Improves brain health and energy
Elinates migraines, lowers depression
Controls epilepsy, autism and alzheimer's

Decreases risk of coronary artery disease

Eliminates chronic pain

Eliminates candida (yeast overgrowth)

Eliminates acne, eczema, psoriasis, rosacea and dandruff

Eliminates sinus issues and asthma

Eliminates acid reflux

Starves cancer cells

Improves fertility and optimizes pregnancy

To start a ketogenic food regimen, you can have a plan and prepare in advance; it way what you consume depends on how early you need to get right into a ketogenic state. How much you restrict your carbohydrates (less than 20g in keeping with day) consumption that a lot speedy you'll input into ketosis mode. The better result will be achieved by lowering your glucose levels.

- Your consumption of nutrients must be around 70% fats, 25% protein, and 5% carbohydrate
- To keep carbs restrained, strive avoiding vegetables, nuts, and dairy product because mainly you may get carbohydrates from them simplest
- Don't consume refined carbohydrates together with wheat (bread, pasta, and cereals), starch (potatoes, beans, legumes) or fruit
- Some of the best choices are dark greens and leafy greens. Mostly your meals ought to be another side of fats with protein and veggies. For instance, chicken breast fried in olive oil, with broccoli and cheese. Steak topped with a knob of butter, and a side of spinach fried in olive oil. If you're still feeling hungry throughout the day, you can seeds, cheeses, snack on nuts or peanut butter to control your appetite.

70%fat

25% protein

5%carbs

Four fundamental steps to begin successfully are:

- Calculate your caloric needed per day, and then add or subtract calories based on your plan
- Set protein intake matching to plan, 0.8 to 1g of protein per pound of lean body mass
- Set carbohydrate intake, around 20-30g according to day (attempt to lower to 20g for the first few weeks, unless exercising)
- Set fats intake primarily based on how many calories you have got left in keeping with day

History of Ketogenic

The ketogenic weight-reduction plan can very well trace its roots to the ancients, in which it was purported that the food plan turned into part of the therapy used to treat epilepsy. Hippocratic medication practitioners, named after the famed doctor of the equal call, believed in treating the epileptic seizures and the accompanying signs and symptoms of epilepsy the usage of dietetic therapy, in which the position of dieting and fasting played a massive part within the fulfillment of the remedy.

This sort of fasting remedy followed for curing many diseases by using historic Indian and Greek physicians and later in 1911, France conducted and used this fasting method as a systematic observe to therapy epilepsy, the food regimen confirmed a few outcomes in affected person's intellectual capacity improvement. Dr. Russel Wilder from Maya Clinic named this fasting weight-reduction plan as a "Ketogenic food regimen" and formally commenced as a treatment for epilepsy.

In the early 1920s, Drs. Cobb and Lennox at Harvard Medical School began to examine the consequences of starvation, and they were the primary to word that seizure development usually befell after 2 or 3 days.

Lennox documented that the manage of seizures happened due to frame metabolism changes through heading off food or much less intake of carbohydrate, this forces the body to burn acid-forming fats. In 1921, Dr. Geyelin turned into the first person inside the American Medical Association convention did test with fasting as a remedy for epilepsy, and he become the primary to file the cognitive improvement that might occur with fasting.

In 1921, Dr.Wilder at the Mayo Clinic defined the advantages of fasting ought to collect if ketonemia produced and he encouraged that a ketogenic weight loss plan (KD) attempted on epilepsy sufferers. He endorsed that the food plan want to be as powerful as fasting and maintained for an longer time. In 1925, Mayo Clinic stated that calculation of Ketogenic Diet for youngsters ought to base on 1 gram of protein in step with kilogram of body weight, 10–15 grams of carbohydrates in step with day, and the the rest of the calories in fats. In amongst 1941 and 1980, Ketogenic Diet has executed prominence inside the textbook on epilepsy in kids's.

This wouldn't be a wonder as the keto weight loss program emphasizes plenty on herbal nutritional fats intake. With this resurgence of a natural dietary choice that modifications the way your body fuels itself, I am happy to be among the people who've benefited from this food regimen. Just read on to get an detail idea!

Types of Ketogenic Diets

If your final aim is not to build muscle, then you can simply skip this section. Usually, every body builder have doubt, is carbs are necessary to build perfect muscle. The ultimate answer is NO; they're now not necessary for the technique muscle building..

Your glycogen stores can nonetheless be reloading whilst on a ketogenic weight-reduction plan. A ketogenic diet is one of the remarkable methods to build muscle, but protein intake performs a essential position here. Especially to gain mass, suggested which you need to be taking in approximately 1 to 1.4g protein per lean pound of body weight. You can obtain your goals through special varieties of a Ketogenic Diet. These are:

Standard Ketogenic Diet (SKD): This is the traditional ketogenic food plan that everyone is aware of and follows. Just we can describe as, a food plan with high in fat, low in carbs and moderate in protein consumption process is called Standard Ketogenic Diet.

- Minimum 20-50 grams of net carbs per day

Targeted Ketogenic Diet (TKD): This is a modification of Standard Ketogenic Diet, but intake of fast digesting carbs earlier than exercise (30-60 minutes) with a high glycemic index to avoid stomach dissatisfied, for exceptional end result cross for glucose and attempt to avoid food items which comprise excessive in fructose. Fructose might fill up liver glycogen as opposed to muscle glycogen, which is essential to prevent on a ketogenic eating regimen. A Targeted Ketogenic Diet offers the platform for keeping exercise performance and permits for glycogen re-synthesis without breaking ketosis for extended intervals of time. Remember, your post exercising food ought to be low in fat and excessive in protein. If you consume fat after exercising, it may lessen muscle recovery and nutrient absorption. So, try to avoid ingesting excessive-fat ingredients after exercise.

- 30-50 grams or less of net carbs
- 30-45 minutes before exercises
- Best for excessive activity and athletes

*Cyclical **Ketogenic Diet (CKD)***: Generally, Cyclical Ketogenic Diet geared toward folks who are doing greater advanced exercising. For instance, body builders and athletes. Cyclical Ketogenic Diet is to empty muscle glycogen between the carb masses absolutely.

- Eating low carbs for few days like 50 carbs per day
- Eating excessive carbs for few days: this is known as the carb loading day with 450-600 grams of carbs intake per day, this lasts for minimum 24 to 48 hours.

CHAPTER 2:
What Happens To Your Body

Going Keto: What Happen To Your Body

When you take more carbohydrates, the body breaks the carbohydrates into glucose to create ATP (Adenosine triphosphate), ATP includes energy to the vicinity where the energy is needed, and once more those ATP is divided into ADP (Adenosine diphosphate) and phosphate, which releases energy depending on reactions. When there is an excess of glucose, it'll be converted to glycogen and saved in the liver and muscular tissues, and additional glycogen might be stored as fat but inside the ketogenic food plan, body (liver) starts off evolved breaking fats by growing fatty acids, and fatty acids broken into a in addition system called as ketogenesis. When the body is within the excessive fats burning mode is called as ketosis. To improve and increase this ketone's, our insulin degree in blood stream have to be small. Using modern's generation, we can measure ketone stages inside the body with serum ketone take a look at. For maximum weight loss, we need to have a serum ketones range amongst 0.5-3mM.

At this point, we've got talked plenty about dietary ketosis and how it is ideal for you, however how do you recognize if you are certainly in a state of nutritional ketosis? This is in which we need to talk approximately how ketones are measured and what are the equipment you can use to measure them. There are three kinds of ketone bodies that we are inquisitive about

- Acetoacetate – the primary body easy found in urine
- Beta-hydroxybutyrate – ketone located in blood
- Acetone – the ketone particles discovered in our breath

Side Effects

When human beings begins a ketogenic eating regimen, they will undergo a few unusual outcomes due to dehydration and insufficient micronutrients inside the body.

Keto flu: Keto flu is one of the common hassle confronted by using keto starters but no need to worry, it's going to depart inside few days, however it is no longer warranty that every person will undergo it. When you are in keto flu transition, you would possibly experience some mild soreness which include a headache, cramps, nausea, fatigue, and many others.

Constipation: Due to dehydration, constipation is common for starters. To keep away from this

- Increase your water intake in line with day from glasses to gallon
- Quality fiber consumption from non-starchy veggies
- Consumption of psyllium husk powder

Cramps: Cramps (especially leg cramps) are a pretty not unusual thing in starters due to loss of minerals and especially because of deficiency of magnesium. It commonly arises within the morning or at night time, however don't worry it is a minor trouble.

- Try to drink greater fluids with little extra salt
- Intake of magnesium supplement

Heart tremor: Heart tremor is commonplace when you are present process a keto transition; you would possibly recognize that your coronary heart is beating more difficult and also faster. Don't fear; you could avoid this with the aid of

- Intake of potassium supplement once per day
- For instantaneous remedy, drink water with little salt

Physical performance: You may sense that your performance on the bed will decrease, this example will be till your body adjust to the use of fat. Once after frame modify, your overall performance might be improved higher than everyday.

Tricks and Tips

Why ketogenic: Before you begin every day, keep in mind and remind yourself approximately first advantages you attain while following a ketogenic weight-reduction plan and tell your self that you may try this for weight reduction and gain health and vitality.

Basic step: Begin every day with a few glasses of water and observed via a cup of detox tea with herbal sweetener which will offer cleansing support for your kidneys and liver for better results.

Supervise: Don't neglect to take measurements and photos earlier than you begin your weight loss plan, this is the first step to screen your progress and take into account this isn't always just for weight loss, that is for accomplishing higher health all through your existence.

Reward: When you reached your weekly aim, reward yourself with an additional smoothie and remind your self approximately notable advantages you gained and going to attain.

Pre-preparation: Depending for your subsequent day timetable you can put together required substances in advance to avoid last minute confusions and additionally you may make a proper recipe primarily based on your interest.

Measuring kit: It is crucial to have size kit to test your every day ketone levels, this allows you find and tune your progress that you are at the right path or want changes to your weight-reduction plan.

Basic Mistakes

More protein consumption: In a ketogenic weight loss plan, we ought to understand ingesting greater protein will result in gluconeogenesis, which converts the amino acids to glucose and ends in boom glucose stages in the body. Just take into account, you need to increase your fats intake.

More nuts intake: Nuts are full of lots of fat however don't forget they have full of masses of calories also. So, try and consume nuts in minimal amount or replace with high-fat end result like Avocado, Coconut, stay, Akee and Durian.

Less fat intake: Remember that intake of fats need to be greater than each protein and carbs. People's consumption of fat is almost equal to protein, however it is wrong, the ratio of consumption have to be 75% fats, 20% protein and 5% carbs.

Same meal: When you are making the identical sort of meal each time, you'll be bored and become bored in reducing. So, to maintain your spirit high, make and discover your recipes with fewer carbs.

Basic Exercises

For any diet, important thing to start a new addiction, as an example, 10-15 mins of body movements per day will assist loads. Let's see a number of the necessary modifications that contribute to losing weight faster while you are on a weight loss program.

Park and stroll: I assume you already heard about this approach, but I am one hundred% sure that this works. Instead of parking in the front of your office or place of work, park little far for subsequent automobile parking space, which makes you walk and lets you proper blood drift to your frame.

Stair case: Instead of the usage of the elevator in an office or every other vicinity, use staircase which squeezes your muscles of the frame and maintains you away from joints, ligaments, and bone pains. Doing like this could burn greater calories.

Shopping: If you do not have a huge shopping listing, then that is the proper time to use your body. Keep the luggage over your shoulders and walk for choosing objects and wearing the heavy grocery gadgets with your fingers is a incredible exercise and the equal time you will be completing your looking for entire weeks also.

Stretching: Sitting in front of your table or laptop is extraordinarily difficult for the body, however there are masses ways that you may work while sitting. One the nice manner is toned your legs at regular intervals and every time you visit the toilet or espresso, stretch your whole frame and move. Upgrade to the stability ball in place of sitting in a normal chair.

Self preparation: Do you recognize that cooking meals by way of yourself for breakfast, lunch, and dinner is also an exercise which facilitates your body and tries to apply extra energy and keep away from destiny health problems?

CHAPTER 3:
Ketogenic Essentials

Remember yourself that ketogenic is high in fats, slight in protein, and really low in carbohydrates. Your nutrient consumption have to be some thing around 75% fats, 20% protein, and 5% carbohydrate.

Mostly in between 20-30g of net carbs is usually recommended for everyday weight-reduction plan however for better result try to the lower your carbohydrate intake and glucose stages. If you're following the ketogenic food regimen for weight loss, it's a great concept to maintain song of each your total carbs and net carbs every day intake.

Protein have to constantly consume as wished with fats by calculating calories consumption consistent with day. You is probably wondering, "What's a net carb?" It's easy! The net carbs are your overall dietary carbohydrates, minus the entire fiber. I definitely suggest you to keep general carbs beneath 35g and net carbs below 25g.

If you're feeling famished inside the course of the day, you may have snacks like nuts, seeds, cheeses, or peanut butter to control your urge for food (this may have an impact to your healthy diet weight reduction plan).

Following a ketogenic diet isn't the perfect problem to deal with, in particular while you don't recognize what you need to consume. Let us see a few critical ketogenic diet meals list to get an concept to make delicious meals recipes with out turning into bored.

Macros

Macros suggest "macronutrients." The 3 primary macronutrients are your each day consumption are fat, proteins, and carbohydrates. All those three vitamins show's one of a kind effects on ketosis from their digestion and feature incidental outcomes on blood glucose and hormones.

Protein and carbs will affect the body from changing into ketosis, but one of the maximum critical component to apprehend is how the ones vitamins are correctly applied for power. These are thru our metabolic pathways after we have received nutrients.

Metabolic pathways: At first, you might be asking yourself what this metabolic pathway is. The manner your body deals with breakdown the fat, proteins, and carbohydrates and makes use of those depending in your state of the body. There are three precise states that your frame undergoes:

- Fed: Immediately after meal
- Fasting: Food consumption delay in between 2-8 hours
- Starved: Food consumption delay for greater than 48 hours

Fats and oil

When you are at the ketogenic weight loss program, fat will play a substantial function on your day by day calorie consumption. Fats are crucial to our bodies, so make sure that you devour right type of fat to avoid incorrect things. The Important Fats that performs a key position in a Ketogenic Diet are:

Saturated fats: These fat are very necessary to keep your immune device wholesome, medical research says that they have no association with threat of heart disease and improve HDL/LDL cholesterol levels.

Polyunsaturated fats: These are commonly available inside the shape of vegetable oils and processed polyunsaturated fat are horrific for the body, so one can get worse HDL/LDL levels of cholesterol and natural polyunsaturated fat are exact for the frame to enhance HDL/LDL cholesterol levels.

Monounsaturated fats: These fat are widely recognized and used for a healthful life-style. These enhance the insulin resistance and better HDL/LDL cholesterol levels. Olive and sunflower oil are examples of healthy monounsaturated fats.

Some of the ketogenic diet foods that are a great source of fats and oils are (mostly prefer organic and grass-fed sources):
- Avocado
- Ghee
- Coconut Oil
- Macadamia Nuts
- Chicken Fat
- Peanut Butter
- Coconut Butter
- Beef tallow
- Butter
- Non-hydrogenated Lard
- Olive Oil
- Mayonnaise (check out for added carbs)
- Red Palm Oil

Protein

Your satisfactory source in relation to protein is deciding on something grass fed or organic and the use of eggs. This will enables to reduce your bacteria and steroid hormone intake.

Fish: Mostly try to eat anything this is caught wild like

- Tuna
- Salmon
- Halibut

- Mackerel
- Catfish
- Mahi-mahi
- Flounder
- Cod
- Snapper
- Trout

Shellfish: Shellfish are low in saturated fat, it contain mostly omega-3 fatty acids and also excellent protein sources, and specifically good sources of zinc, iron, copper and vitamin B-12

- Crab
- Mussels
- Oysters
- Lobster
- Squid
- Scallops

Whole eggs: If feasible, attempt to get free-range/organic eggs from the local market. You can prepare them in extraordinary approaches and styles like

- Boiled
- Poached
- Fried
- Scrambled

Poultry: Coming to poultry, they are low in calories and high in protein, which makes it ideal for weight maintenance and perfectly fits in keto diet (best option could be free range or organic)

- Chicken
- Duck
- Quail
- Pheasant

Meat: Mostly grass fed are desired because they have a better fatty acid

- Beef
- Veal
- Goat
- Lamb
- Wild meat

Pork: It is excessive in protein and important vitamins, minerals and amino acid perfect for fitness, trim of visible fat, is nutrient-dense, satisfying, and good for you. Some red meat elements like that of tenderloin, loin chops and sirloin roast are made from the lean cuts and are greater values than chicken. Mainly check for added sugars.

- Pork chops
- Pork loin
- Ham

Peanut butter: Get natural and herbal peanut butter, but be cautious as they have got immoderate counts of carbohydrates and Omega-6s. If you need, you could switch to macadamia nut butter.

Vegetables

While on a ketogenic weight loss plan, try and get veggies that develop above the ground and sparkling leafy veggies (mostly prefer organic) however if you can't get them don't fear. Research studies show that organic and non-organic greens still have the equal nutritional values and traits. Always try to keep away from starchy veggies like:

- Peas
- Corn
- Yucca
- Legumes
- Parsnips
- Beans
- Potatoes
- Yams

Seeds/Nuts

Roasted seeds and nuts and seeds are high-quality to remove any anti-vitamins. If possible, generally avoid peanuts; truly, they may come below legumes, no longer encouraged inside the ketogenic weight loss plan meals listing.

- Almonds, walnuts, and macadamias are the best regarding your carbs count, and you could eat in small quantities to decrease carbs consumption
- Pistachios and cashews are higher in carbs so make that you matter them cautiously even as eating
- Bsically, nuts are high in Omega 6 Fatty Acids, Avoid over consumption
- Seed and nut flours are the great substitute for regular flour, such as almond flour and milled flax seed will be the best choice

Beverages

The ketogenic diet has a natural diuretic impact, so dehydration is common within the strategy planning stage of weight loss program for most people. If you're vulnerable to urinary tract infections or bladder pain, you have to be mainly organized for it. Usually, we're presupposed to drink eight glasses of in regular basis.

- Water (as needed)
- Coffee
- Herbal Tea

Sweeteners

Staying away from sweet items is the exceptional wager. It will assist manipulate your cravings to a minimal degree, which particularly contributes to achieving success at the ketogenic weight loss plan. If you want to have a sweets prefer artificial sweetener. Try to move for liquid sweeteners, which include

- Liquid stevia
- Xylitol
- Erythritol
- Liquid Sucralose
- Monk Fruit

CHAPTER 4:
Overview Of Ketogenic Food

Ketogenic Protein Source

Your quality wager with regards to protein is selecting pasture-raised and grass-fed. This will minimize your micro organism and steroid hormone intake. Try to pick the darker meat where feasible with poultry, as it's far a great deal fattier than white meat. Eating fatty fish is a amazing way to get omega 3's in as nicely.

When it comes to pork, there's not too much to avoid. Cured meats and sausages can from time to time have introduced sugars and delivered processed ingredients. If you consume steak, try and choose fattier cuts like ribeye. If you like hamburger meat (ground red meat), try to select fattier ratios like 80/20 in a few instances.

One aspect you do need to be careful of whilst coping with meat is your protein intake t. Too a great deal protein on a ketogenic food regimen can result in decrease ranges of ketone manufacturing and elevated production of glucose. You want to intention for dietary ketosis.

Try to balance out the protein for your food with fattier aspect dishes and sauces. If you pick out to consume lean red meat, you have to be in particular cautious with the portioning of protein. Jerky and different red meat snacks can add up in protein very speedy, so make certain to pair it with something fatty – like cheese!

If you don't devour pork or red meat, you could always alternative lamb in its location considering the fact that it is very fatty. Replace cuts of meat like bacon with similar, leaner items. Add more fats if wanted.

Protein Source	Calories	Protein (g)
Bacon, 1 slice (~ 8g), baked	44	2.9
Beef, Sirloin Steak, 1 ounce, broiled	69	7.7
Beef, Ground, 5% fat, 1 ounce, broiled	44	6.7
Beef, Ground, 15% fat, 1 ounce, broiled	70	7.2
Beef, Ground, 30% fat, 1 ounce, broiled	77	7.1
Beef, Bottom Round, 1 ounce, roasted	56	7.6
Chicken, white meat, 1 ounce	49	8.8
Chicken, dark meat, 1 ounce	58	7.8
Egg, 1 large, 50 g	72	6.3
Fish, Raw, Cod, 1 ounce	20	4.3
Fish, Raw, Flounder, 1 ounce	20	3.5
Fish, Raw, Sole, 1 ounce	20	3.5
Fish, Raw, Salmon, 1 ounce	40	5.6
Ham, smoked, 1 ounce	50	6.4
Hot dog, beef, 1 ounce	92	3.1
Lamb, ground, 1 ounce, broiled	80	7
Lamb chop, boneless, 1 ounce, broiled	67	7.3
Pork chop, bone-in, 1 ounce, broiled	65	6.7

Pork ribs, ribs, 1 ounce, roasted	102	6.2
Scallops, 1 ounce, steamed	31	5.8
Shrimp, 1 ounce, cooked	28	6.8
Tuna, 1 ounce, cooked	52	8.5
Turkey Breast, 1 ounce, roasted	39	8.4
Veal, roasted, 1 ounce	42	8

Ketogenic Vegetable Source

Vegetables are a paramount a part of a wholesome keto food plan, but occasionally we're caught with choices we would remorse later. Some veggies are excessive in sugar and don't cut it nutritionally – so we want to weed them out.

The first select veggies for a ketogenic food plan are excessive in vitamins and low in carbohydrates. These, as most of you could wager, are dark and leafy. Anything that resembles spinach or kale will fall into this category and will be the nice issue to include in something you may.

Try to go after cruciferous greens which can be grown above floor, leafy, and green. If you may opt for organic as there are fewer pesticide residues, however if you may't then don't fear. Studies show that organic and non-organic vegetables still have the identical nutritional traits. Both frozen and fresh vegetables are desirable to consume.

Vegetables that grow under ground can nevertheless be fed on sparsely – you just ought to be cautious about the variety of carbs that they've. Usually, underground veggies can be used for flavor (like 1/2 an red onion for a whole pot of soup) and effortlessly moderated.

Basically, there's no fitting rule that works flawlessly. Try to pick your greens with carbohydrates in thoughts and component them based totally on their carb counts.

Protein Source	Calories	Carbs (g)
Bacon, 1 slice (~ 8g), baked	44	0
Beef, Sirloin Steak, 1 ounce, broiled	69	0
Beef, Ground, 5% fat, 1 ounce, broiled	44	0
Beef, Ground, 15% fat, 1 ounce, broiled	70	0
Beef, Ground, 30% fat, 1 ounce, broiled	77	0
Beef, Bottom Round, 1 ounce, roasted	56	0
Chicken, white meat, 1 ounce	49	0
Chicken, dark meat, 1 ounce	58	0
Egg, 1 large, 50 g	72	0.4
Fish, Raw, Cod, 1 ounce	20	0
Fish, Raw, Flounder, 1 ounce	20	0
Fish, Raw, Sole, 1 ounce	20	0
Fish, Raw, Salmon, 1 ounce	40	0
Ham, smoked, 1 ounce	50	0
Hot dog, beef, 1 ounce	92	0.5
Lamb, ground, 1 ounce, broiled	80	0
Lamb chop, boneless, 1 ounce, broiled	67	0

Pork chop, bone-in, 1 ounce, broiled	65	0
Pork ribs, ribs, 1 ounce, roasted	102	0
Scallops, 1 ounce, steamed	31	1.5
Shrimp, 1 ounce, cooked	28	0
Tuna, 1 ounce, cooked	52	0
Turkey Breast, 1 ounce, roasted	39	0
Veal, roasted, 1 ounce	42	0

Ketogenic Diary Source

Dairy is normally ate up in tandem with food on keto. Try to hold your dairy intake to a moderate mode. Most of your food should be coming from protein, greens, and introduced fat/cooking oils.

Raw and organic dairy items are favored right here, if to be had. Highly processed dairy generally has wide variety of carbohydrates as raw/organic dairy so it does add up over the years. Make sure to choose complete fat products over free fats or low in fat as they'll have appreciably greater carbs and much less "filling" effects.

If you have got lactose sensitivities, stay with very hard and aged dairy products as they comprise tons less lactose. Some examples of dairy you can devour on keto are:

Diary Source	Calories	Fats (g)	Carbs (g)
Buttermilk, whole, 1 ounce	18	0.9	1.4
Cheese, Blue, 1 ounce	100	8.2	0.7
Cheese, Brie, 1 ounce	95	7.9	0.1
Cheese, Cheddar, 1 ounce	114	9.4	0.4
Cheese, Colby, 1 ounce	110	9	0.7
Cheese, Cottage, 2%, 1 ounce	24	0.7	1
Cheese, Cream, block, 1 ounce	97	9.7	1.1
Cheese, Feta, 1 ounce	75	6	1.2
Cheese, Monterey Jack, 1 ounce	106	8.6	0.2
Cheese, Mozzarella, whole milk, 1 oz	85	6.3	0.6
Cheese, Parmesan, hard, 1 ounce	111	7.3	0.9
Cheese, Swiss, 1 ounce	108	7.9	1.5
Cheese, Mascarpone, 1 ounce	130	13	1
Cream, half-n-half, 1 ounce	39	3.5	1.3
Cream, heavy, 1 ounce	103	11	0.8
Cream, Sour, full fat, 1 ounce	55	5.6	0.8
Milk, whole, 1 ounce	19	1	1.5
Milk, 2%, 1 ounce	15	0.6	1.5
Milk, skim, 1 ounce	10	0	1.5

Ketogenic Seeds and Nuts Source

Nuts and seeds are good when they're roasted to take away any anti-vitamins. Try to keep away from peanuts if possible, as they are legumes which aren't quite permitted within the ketogenic food plan food listing.

Typically raw nuts can be used to feature flavorings or texture to food. Some human beings select to consume them as snacks – which may be rewarding but may work against weight reduction dreams. Snacking will enhance insulin degrees and lead to slower weight loss inside the long term.

Nuts may be a fantastic supply of fat, but you usually should take into account that they do have carbohydrate counts which can add up speedy. It's also especially essential to note that they do comprise protein as properly. Nut flours particularly can upload up in protein instead speedy – so be cautious of the amount you use.

Nuts can also be high in omega 6 fatty acids, so it's proper to be cautious with the amount you consume. For standard eating, you need to stick with fattier and lower carbohydrate nuts.

Nuts/Seed Source	Calories	Fats (g)	Protein (g)
Almonds, raw, 1 ounce	170	15	6
Brazil Nuts, raw, 1 ounce	186	19	4
Cashews, raw, 1 ounce	160	13	5
Chestnuts, raw, 1 ounce	55	0	0
Chia Seeds, raw, 1 ounce	131	10	7
Coconut, dried, unsweetened, 1 ounce	65	6	1
Flax Seeds, raw, 1 ounce	131	10	7
Hazelnuts, raw, 1 ounce	176	17	4
Macadamia Nuts, raw, 1 ounce	203	21	2
Peanuts, raw, 1 ounce	157	13	7
Pecans, raw, 1 ounce	190	20	3
Pine Nuts, raw, 1 ounce	189	20	4
Pistachios, raw, 1 ounce	158	13	6
Pumpkin Seeds, raw, 1 ounce	159	14	8
Sesame Seeds, raw, 1 ounce	160	14	5
Sunflower Seeds, raw, 1 ounce	150	11	3
Walnuts, raw, 1 ounce	185	18	4

Ketogenic Sweeteners

Staying away from anything sweet tasting is the first choice, it'll assist slash your cravings to a minimum stage, which basically promotes success at the ketogenic weight loss plan. If you have to have some thing sweet, although, there are a few alternatives available to choose from.

When searching for sweeteners, try to move after liquid variations as they don't have introduced binders (maltodextrin and dextrose). These are typically discovered in blends like

Splenda and may add up in carbs very, very quickly. For keto, you want to attempt to stay with decrease glycemic index sweeteners.

Please observe that this is only a small listing of sweeteners that humans use on keto. There's heaps of various manufacturers and blends accessible – we regularly use a aggregate of stevia and erythritol in our dessert recipes. You can also find something that suits your tastes better, although, simply ensure that it's miles at the desirable sweetener listing.

Typically you want to live away from any brands that use filler substances like maltodextrin and dextrose, or excessive glycemic sweeteners like maltitol. Many low-carb products that declare low net carbs generally use these sugar alcohols. Many goodies which can be "free sugar" additionally use these sweeteners. Avoid them wherein possible. These precise sweeteners respond in our body in a comparable way sugar does.

When a sweetener has a low glycemic impact (or a low glycemic index), it has little impact on blood sugar. The higher the glycemic index is, the better your blood sugar will spike at some point of consumption. Here's our encouraged list of 0 GI sweeteners:

Sweetener	Net Carbs (Per 100g)	Calories (Per 100g)
Sucralose	0	0
Stevia	5	20
Erythritol	5	20
Xylitol	60	240
Aspartame	85	352

Low Carb Vegetables

The first selecting veggies for a ketogenic food plan are excessive in vitamins and low in carbohydrates upon that below you can find very lo-carb vegetable list, which you regularly use over time or until you finish your diet plan. These, as most of you could wager, are dark and leafy. Anything that resembles spinach or kale will fall into this category and will be the nice issue to include in something you may.

Vegetable	Amount	Net Carbs
Mustard Greens	1/2 Cup	0.1
Parsley (Chopped)	1/2 Cup	0.1
Spinach (Raw)	1/2 Cup	0.1
Bok Choi	1/2 Cup	0.2
Endive	1/2 Cup	0.2
Lettuce (Iceberg)	1/2 Cup	0.2
Lettuce (Romaine)	1/2 Cup	0.2
Sprouts Alfalfa	1/2 Cup	0.2
Lettuce (Boston Bibb)	1/2 Cup	0.4
Turnip Greens (Boiled)	1/2 Cup	0.6
Radicchio	1/2 Cup	0.7

Broccoli florets	1/2 Cup	0.8
Cauliflower (Steamed)	1/2 Cup	0.9
Garlic (Fresh)	1 Clove	0.9
Radishes	10	0.9
Zucchini, cooked	1/2 Cup	1
Cucumber (Raw)	1/2 Cup	1
Nopalo (Grilled)	1/2 Cup	1
Pepper (Jalepeno)	1/2 Cup	1
Cabbage (Green Raw)	1/2 Cup	1.1
Mushroom (Shitake Cooked)	1/2 Cup	1.1
Squash (Summer)	1/2 Cup	1.3
Cabbage (Red Raw)	1/2 Cup	1.4
Cauliflower (Raw)	1/2 Cup	1.4
Mushroom (Button)	1/2 Cup	1.4
Squash (Zucchini Steamed)	1/2 Cup	1.5
Asparagus (Steamed)	4 Spears	1.6
Cabbage (Green Steamed)	1/2 Cup	1.6
Fennel fresh	1/2 Cup	1.8
Cabbage (Savoy Steamed)	1/2 Cup	1.9
Artichoke (Hearts)	4 Pieces	2
Broccoli Rabe	1/2 Cup	2
Collard Greens	1/2 Cup	2
Bean Sprouts	1/2 Cup	2.1
Eggplant (Broiled)	1/2 Cup	2.1
Kale steamed	1/2 Cup	2.1
Sauerkraut	1/2 Cup	2.1
Spinach (Steamed)	1/2 Cup	2.2
Tomato (Plum)	1	2.2
Turnips (Boiled)	1/2 Cup	2.3
Scallions	1/2 Cup	2.4
Jicama (Raw)	1/2 Cup	2.5
Tomato (Tomatillo)	1/2 Cup	2.6
Green Beans steamed	1/2 Cup	2.9
Yellow Wax Beans	1/2 Cup	2.9
Celery (Raw)	1 Stem	3
Peas (Snow)	1/2 Cup	3.4
Pepper (Green Bell)	1/2 Cup	3.5
Pepper (Red Bell)	1/2 Cup	3.5
Okra (Steamed)	1/2 Cup	3.8
Mushroom (Portobello)	4oz.	4.1
Pumpkin (Canned)	1/2 Cup	4.1
Pumpkin (Boiled)	1/2 Cup	4.6
Brussels Sprouts (Steamed)	1/2 Cup	4.7

Okra (Fried)	1/2 Cup	4.8
Onion (Chopped)	1/2 Cup	5.5
Carrot (Steamed)	1 Large	5.6
Rutabaga	1/2 Cup	5.9
Tomato (Cherry)	10	6
Carrot (Raw)	1 Large	6.5
Peas (Regular)	1/2 Cup	6.5
Broccoli	1/2 Cup	6.7
Artichoke (Whole)	1 Whole	6.9
Water chestnuts	1/2 Cup	7
Squash (Spaghetti)	1/2 Cup	7.8
Squash (Butternut Baked)	1/2 Cup	7.9
Squash (Acorn Baked)	1/2 Cup	10.4
Fava Beans	1/2 Cup	12.1
Parsnips (Steamed)	1/2 Cup	12.1
Corn (Kernels)	1/2 Cup	12.6
Shallots	1/2 Cup	12.9
Corn (Whole Cob)	Whole Cob	17.2
Yucca (Steamed)	1/2 Cup	26
Yuca fresh	1/2 Cup	37.2

CHAPTER 5:
Going Keto: Good and Bad

Ketosis Finding

You recognise ketogenic diets are a extraordinary manner to lose and hold body weight and the trade in lifestyle are complete of incredible blessings (already discussed in the preceding earlier chapters). If observed continually and correctly, keto diets make your body ruin down fats to ketones, so as to be used as strength fuels. While on a keto weight loss plan, your body will undergo a few organic diversification and/or modifications, with a purpose to result in the outcrop of a few symptoms. These signs and symptoms normally disappear whilst your body is keto-tailored. The idea for this unique step is such that with the fore information of what might be taking place to your frame as you go in ketosis, it would be capable of assist you to maintain the weight loss plan with a peace of thoughts. After all, they do say knowledge is energy.

There are some shortcuts and hints to attaining ultimate ketosis. Optimal Ketosis can flawlessly end thru nutritional nutrition on my own. Instant of the usage of some misguided tools, you may find with easy bodily "signs and symptoms" that typically will let you recognize in case you're on right track or not

Increased Urination: Keto is a herbal diuretic, so if you are going to the bathroom extra regularly than normal then it is one of the signs that you are in right track. These are specifically because of elimination of a ketone frame from body through urination, lead to more rest room visits for beginners

Dry Mouth: The ordinary urination leads to dry mouth and increases thirst. Make sure that you're drinking plenty of required water (gallon) and supplement your electrolytes (salt, potassium, magnesium)

Bad Breath: Acetone is a ketone body that in part removed via your breath. It can scent sharp like over ripe fruit (much like nail polish remover). It's handiest temporary for beginners and is goes away after some time

Increased energy/Reduced hunger: Normally, after passing "keto flu," you'll experience and experience lower in starvation mode, and this mode is referred to as energized mental state

Tiredness (only for short period): This symptom is a completely commonplace and unsightly one for first-time keto dieters. The feel of fatigue makes people feeling dissatisfied and that they prevent halfway earlier than the body receives a chance to get into a entire ketosis mode. Such humans are unable to obtain the mammoth blessings of ketogenic diets.

Keto flu: This is some soreness which could increase from a myriad of symptoms which may also consist of emotions of lightheadedness, constipation, headaches, diarrhea as well as carb cravings. This collectively is called the keto flu, which is understood to afflict some individuals who start off at the ketogenic diet. This can also were the single most essential cause why humans declare that the food regimen does no longer paintings for them, seeing as that they revel in negative effects as soon as the weight loss program began.

Typically, those symptoms last no various weeks,with a few humans no longer getting them at all, and others just popping out of it after some days. If you do locate your self constantly feeling like this, it can be a sign that your body is failing to get into ketosis.

At this juncture, we would must pass lower back to the fundamentals and begin searching at the quantity of carbs and proteins in addition to fat you are consuming. Chances are that there has been an over intake of carbs or underneath intake of fat or each. Once we get them taken care of out, these emotions of soreness must go off and it is time to chill and experience the advantages of being in regular ketosis.

Ketosis Testing

There are different of domestic kits that help to locate and find out ketones tiers inside the body. Some of them are:

Breathalyzer: These are one of the most inexpensive ways to locate ketone concentrations inside the body. Normally, while you are on the ketogenic eating regimen, your breath may have a distinct smell, that is particularly due to acetones.

Ketone strips: Urine ketone strips are one of the different reasonably priced and easy ways to locate an extra of ketone our bodies might be excreted from the body in urine, but this isn't so effective.

Ketone meter: The blood ketone meter is one of the satisfactory and effective methods to locate ketone degrees within the body, it's far little costly, but you may display your ketone stages on a each day foundation for the entire weight loss in much less length.

Self-attention: You can hear or concentrate from your body, for instance: by means of your distinguishable breath, trade in urine color and fruity sweat odor. If you locate these modifications in you, then you definitely're in ketosis

CHAPTER 6:
Guide to Start Your Ketogenic Journey

Part 1: The Beginning

Step 1: Talk and get suggestions from your doctor

Step 2: Identify and recognize most possible risks of a ketogenic diet

Step 3: Start with low-carb diet to ease yourself into nutritional ketosis

Step 4: Calculate daily macronutrients intake details

Part 2: Adjusting and Modifying

Step 5: Minimum intake of carbs per day is 20-30 grams

Step 6: minimum intake of protein several times per day is 2–8 oz

Step 7: Fat fat fat ….fat more fats with all your meals

Step 8: Don't think much about and don't stress too much about calories intake

Step 9: More hydrated

Part 3: Losing Weight

Step 10: Regular check on ketosis using a keto meter and other keto testing analyzers

Step 11: Kketo flu

Step 12: Check your health has improved or not (after a few weeks)

CHAPTER 7:
14 Day Ketogenic Diet Meal Plan

Week 1 Guide

Our number one motive is quite simple in the first week. At the primary week, you don't want to do difficult transition due to the fact it's far very difficult sincerely to take away your food cravings. We are going to bear in mind leftovers things, due to the fact why to cook identical food over and over? Breakfast is some component I commonly prepare dinner with leftover objects, in which I don't should worry for morning and no want to suppose and sense strain about it.

The first signs that you are moving into ketosis are called the "keto flu" wherein headaches, fatigue, mind fogginess, and so forth can disturb your frame. Make certain and do not forget to consuming plenty of water with salt (I propose a gallon in step with day). The ketogenic diet plan is a natural diuretic, and also you'll be peeing extra than regular. Take underneath consideration that you're peeing out electrolytes, and you can wager that you'll be having an full-size headache no time. Make positive that your salt consumption and water intake excessive enough than normal, to allow your body to re-hydrate and re-supply your electrolytes.

Breakfast

For breakfast, you need to thing about easy, tasty, and leftovers I advise beginning day 1 want to be at the weekend. This way, you may make some thing that allows you to final you for the complete week. The first week is all approximately simple.

Lunch

Lunch goes to be smooth. Normally, it'll be salad and meat, unfold in high-fat dressings. If you are not feeling like making, you could use leftover meat from previous nights or use easy available canned bird/fish. If you do use canned meats, ensure which you study apparently the label for hidden carbs. Additionally, you could additionally add spices and seasonings on your salad to your liking. Just be careful approximately garlic and onion powder, but special spices can have negligible carbs.

Dinner

Dinner goes to be a mixture of leafy vegetables (huge broccoli and spinach) with a few meat. Remember, we are going to immoderate fat and slight protein consumption.

Note: Don't forget to drink water (plenty) with little salt.

DAY	BREAKFAST	LUNCH	SNACK	DINNER
Day 1	Pepper Omelet	Mixed Squash Salad	Sesame Cabbage Biscuits	Turkey Summer Zoodles
Day 2	Bacon Coconut Pancakes	Bacon Broccoli Soup	Durian Mug Cake	Turkey Ghee Soup

Day 3	Chicken Avocado Rolls	Arugula Avocado Bowl	Heavy Banana Bombs	Chicken Dill Salad
Day 4	Berry Bread	Turkey Ghee Soup	Ripe Avocado Smoothie	Sweet Cheese Duck Salad
Day 5	Chia Broccoli Pancakes	Turkey Salad	Heavy Banana Bombs	Winter Vegetable Stew
Day 6	Stuffed Eggs	Cabbage Cheddar Soup	Mexican Cream Smoothie	Cabbage Cheese Meal
Day 7	Fat Rich Broccoli	Almond Kimchi Bowl	Crunchy Flax Biscuits	Layered Asparagus Lamb

Week 2 Guide

Wow, already week 1 is finished successfully. I wish you're nevertheless doing well on a diet and have found an easy way to keep track with high spirit. Again these week, we're going to maintain simple breakfast. We're going to introduce keto coffee. It's a mixed with coconut oil, butter, and heavy cream in your coffee. When you blend the oil, butter, and cream collectively, it simply adds an effete richness to your espresso that I am pretty confident which you'll adore it.

Breakfast

For breakfast, we will change a little bit and will introduce Keaton coffee. I know some people gained like it. If you don't like coffee, then attempt herbal tea.

Why keto coffee?

Fat loss: Clean and easy, the consumption of medium-chain triglycerides (MCT) has been proven to result in greater losses in fat tissue (adipose tissue), in both animals and human beings.

Fat: Fat intake ends in an full-size amounts of strength, efficient usage of body energy, and extra efficient manner to weight loss faster than a everyday eating regimen (it's the main aspect of this food regimen).

Energy: Researchers have proven that the speedy rate of oxidation in Medium Chain Fatty Acids (MCFAs) results in an increase in energy. Mainly, MCFAs are transformed into ketones, are absorbed in another way in the body compared to everyday oils, and produces more energy. Feel unfastened to add sweetener and spices (cinnamon, stevia, vanilla extract) to this if you're not the most important fan of the sweet taste.

Lunch

We're going to maintain simple and assimilate more meat. Green vegetables fry or soups and high-fats dressings are crucial objects. Keep track of fats and protein intake due to the fact taking proper amount is crucial.

Dinner

Dinner is quite easy. Meats, vegetables, high-fat dressings are important for keto. Don't over assume a lot approximately weight reduction within the first 2 weeks; honest and steady facilitates to reach your desired goal.

DAY	BREAKFAST	LUNCH	SNACK	DINNER
Day 8	Feta Wraps	Smoked Salmon Salad	Energy Peanut Bars	Lamb Sausage Soup
Day 9	Zucchini Sausage Casserole	Creamy Veggie Soup	Chia Banana Smoothie	Roasted Walnut Tuna Filet
Day 10	Cheese Cabbage Casserole	Red Chard Cheese Soup	Protein Flax Bars	Wild Salmon Soup
Day 11	Chicken Pots	Ghee Rind Balls	Chocolate Pie	Pepper Turkey Soup
Day 12	Mascarpone Avocado	Grilled Mascarpone Salmon	Cream Pots	Brazil Sea Bass
Day 13	Cabbage Bread	Green Nut Salad	Coco Seed Smoothie	Coconut Turkey Stew
Day 14	Stuffed Eggs	Lamb Sausage Soup	Cream Pots	Cabbage Cheddar Soup

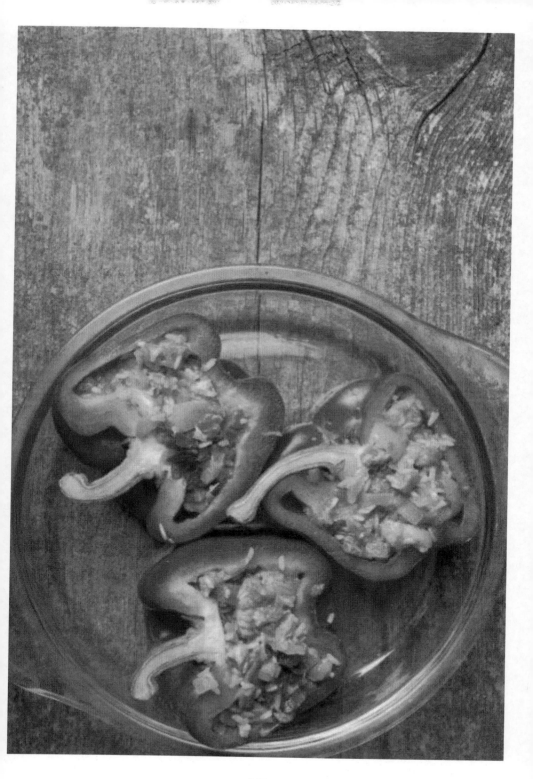

-43

CHAPTER 8:
Ketogenic Diet Recipes

Breakfast Recipes

Recipe 1: Berry Bread

Ingredients
Bread

- Stevia 2 tbsp.
- Ghee 2 tbsp.
- Egg 1
- Egg yolk 2
- Orange juice 2 tsp.
- Berry extracts 1 tsp.
- Almond flour 0.5 oz.
- Baking powder ½ tsp.
- Chia flour 2 tsp.
- Pinch of salt

Berry Glaze

- Ghee 2 tbsp.
- Berries 1 oz.
- Erythritol 3 tbsp.

Preparation Method
1. At first, preheat the oven to 350F. In a mixing bowl, add all bread ingredients together and mix well until it forms nice batter.
2. Line a baking sheet with parchment paper and put batter (if desired, you can create your own bread shape).
3. Place in a preheated oven and bake for 10 minutes and let it cool for 5 minutes.
4. Meanwhile, prepare glaze by adding all ingredients in a small bowl and mix using hand mixer.
5. Put this glaze in the fridge for minimum 30 minutes, using spoon, gently glaze your bread and enjoy the taste.

Nutritional Information
- Preparation Time: 15 minutes
- Total servings: 2
- Calories: 189 (per serving)
- Fat: 17.1g
- Protein: 7.9g
- Carbs: 2.4g

Recipe 2: Mascarpone Avocado

Ingredients

- Eggs yolk 2
- Eggs white 3
- Almond flour 2 tbsp.
- Ricotta cheese 3.5 oz.
- Mascarpone cheese 1 oz.
- Fruit extract ½ tsp.
- Ghee 1 tbsp.
- Cream of tartar ½ tsp.
- Baking soda ¼ tsp.
- Avocado 2.5 oz.
- Stevia 10 drops

Preparation Method

1. At first, preheat your oven to 350F. In a separate bowl add egg yolks, vanilla extract, ricotta cheese, mascarpone and stevia.
2. Other side beat egg whites with baking soda and cream of tartar until they become thick and form soft peaks.
3. Now add egg white's mixture to egg yolk mixture and very gently fold in and slowly add the almond flour.
4. Place the sliced avocado onto a baking dish lined with parchment paper and greased with ghee.
5. Top with the pancake mixture and add more avocado on top. Spray with ghee and place in preheated oven. Set timer to 15 minutes until slightly browned and serve warm.

Nutritional Information

- Preparation Time: 25 minutes
- Total servings: 2
- Calories: 353 (per serving)
- Fat: 26.9g
- Protein: 14.6g
- Carbs: 5.8g

Recipe 3: Chia Broccoli Pancakes

Ingredients

- Chia meal 1 cup
- Large eggs 2
- Maple syrup 1 tbsp.
- Broccoli puree 2 fl oz.
- Cream ¼ cup
- Ghee 2 tbsp.
- All spice 1 tsp.
- Baking soda ½ tsp.
- Salt to taste

Preparation Method

1. Mix eggs, broccoli puree, maple, cream and ghee together without lumps.
2. Mix chia meal, all spice, baking soda and salt together in separate bowl.
3. Slowly start adding wet mixture (step1) to get smooth consistency by adding butter.
4. Heat the pan and grease the pan with butter, then add the pancake batter into the pan and cook until bubbles appears on the top.
5. Flip it and cook other side until browned and serve when it is warm for a nice taste.

Nutritional Information

- Preparation Time: 15 minutes
- Total servings: 8
- Calories: 191 (per serving)
- Fat: 16.4g
- Protein: 8g
- Carbs: 4g

Recipe 4: Zucchini Sausage Casserole

Ingredients

- Sausage 1 lb.
- Zucchini 0.5 lb.
- Broccoli 0.5 lb.
- Red onions 1.5 oz.
- Large eggs 3
- Ghee 2 tbsp.
- Mayonnaise ½ cup
- Mustard seeds 1 ½ tsp.
- Mascarpone cheese 6 oz
- Red pepper flakes to taste
- Dill 1 tbsp.

Preparation Method

1. At first, preheat your oven to 375F and grease a casserole dish with ghee and keep aside.
2. In large skillet, cook sausage in a medium heat for 10 minutes. Add broccoli, zucchini and red onions, cook until vegetables are tender and sausage is fully cooked.
3. In separate bowl, mix eggs, mayonnaise, mustard and pepper until smooth. Add grated cheese to egg mixture and stir. Add this mixture to casserole dish and top it with little extra cheese.
4. Bake for 30 minutes in a preheated oven or until bubbling around the edges. After 30 minutes, remove from oven, add ghee and serve immediately.

Nutritional Information

- Preparation Time: 40 minutes
- Total servings: 6
- Calories: 478 (per serving)
- Fat: 40.1g
- Protein: 16.6g
- Carbs: 5.5g

Recipe 5: Chicken Pots

Ingredients

Crust:

- Almond flour 4 oz.
- Coconut flour 2 oz.
- Baking powder 2 tsp.
- Pink salt ¼ tsp.
- Dill ¼ tsp.
- Egg 1
- Mozzarella cheese 12 oz.
- Ghee 6 oz.

Filling:

- Chicken breast 1 lb.
- Ghee 2 tbsp.
- Carrot 1 oz.
- Coriander leaves ¼ tsp.
- Vinegar 1 tbsp.
- Heavy cream 4 oz.
- Peas 1 oz.
- Paprika 2 tsp.
- Salt and pepper to taste

Preparation Method

1. At first, preheat your oven to 350F then grease your muffin or cupcakes with ghee.
2. Now, we can make filling by placing pan over medium heat and add ghee. When ghee is hot then add diced chicken and cook until it roasted.
3. Add remaining all ingredients and cook for 15 minutes then keep aside.
4. Now you can start making crust, by mixing all crust ingredients one by one in log shape. It should be soft then divide it into 12 equal parts.
5. Roll each piece and place two rolls on each other than press over muffin tins.
6. Now, fill the muffins cups with cooled filling and top with one more roll.
7. Finally place in preheated oven and cook for 25 minutes or until you find golden brown on top of muffins.
8. Let it cool for 5 minutes and enjoy the taste with your family.

Nutritional Information

- Preparation Time: 45 minutes
- Total servings: 4
- Calories: 444 (per serving)
- Fat: 41g
- Protein: 18.1g
- Carbs: 6.4g

Recipe 6: Stuffed Eggs

Ingredients

- Eggs 6 (boiled)
- Soy sauce ½ cup
- Water 1 cup
- Vinegar 30ml
- Garlic powder 1 tsp.
- Cream cheese 4 oz.
- Thyme 1 tbsp.
- All spice 1 tsp.
- Ghee 2 tbsp.
- Salt and black pepper to taste

Preparation Method

1. At first, mix water, soy sauce, vinegar, garlic powder in a small bowl and keep aside.
2. Soak the eggs in sauce and refrigerate for 2 hours then cut into half and egg yolks separately.
3. Now mix egg yolk, cream, thyme, salt and pepper in a mixing bowl then stuff into egg white.
4. Finally, sprinkle all spice powder over it then add ghee over every piece and enjoy the delicious taste.

Nutritional Information

- Preparation Time: 15 minutes
- Total servings: 4
- Calories: 236 (per serving)
- Fat: 24.1g
- Protein: 12g
- Carbs: 3.4g

Recipe 7: Cheese Cabbage Casserole

Ingredients

Puree

- White cabbage 1
- Heavy cream 2 tbsp.
- Ghee 1 tbsp.
- Cheddar cheese 1 oz.
- All spice ½ tbsp.
- Garlic powder 1 tsp.
- Salt and pepper to taste

Layer

- Cream cheese 6 oz.
- Cheddar cheese 2 oz.
- Salsa sauce 1 oz.

Topping

- Parmashen cheese 2.5 oz.
- Fresh basil 2 tbsp.

Preparation Method

1. Make puree, blend the cabbage, cheese, all spice, garlic, and salt, pepper using a blender and put in a bowl. Add cream, ghee, and place in microwave oven for 10 minutes on high and keep aside.
2. Now, make layer by placing cream cheese, shredded cheese, salsa in a microwave safe bowl for 30 seconds until cheese soften.
3. In a large bowl make casserole by spread cabbage puree spread the warm layer mixture on top of the puree, top with a layer of shredded Parmesan cheese and sprinkle fresh basil over it.
4. Place in oven and bake for 20 minutes at 375F and enjoy delicious taste with your friends or family.

Nutritional Information

- Preparation Time: 35 minutes
- Total servings: 6
- Calories: 333.5 (per serving)
- Fat: 28.6g
- Protein: 13.5g
- Carbs: 4.2g

Recipe 8: Chia Milk Pancakes

Ingredients

- Almond flour ½ cup
- Chia meal ½ cup
- Large eggs 4
- Maple syrup 2 tbsp.
- Avocado oil 4 tsp.
- Coconut milk ½ cup
- Stevia 4 tsp.
- Ghee 2 tbsp.
- Coconut flour 1 tsp.
- Cinnamon ½ tsp.
- Salt to taste

Topping:

- Mixed dry cherries 2 tbsp.

Preparation Method

1. At first, mix almond flour, chia seeds, stevia, salt and baking powder in bowl.
2. Mix all dry ingredients together well so everything is distributed evenly and add eggs to mixture and mix well.
3. Mix to a liquid consistency is achieved and add now avocado oil, maple syrup and milk together and mix until more liquid consistency.
4. Add coconut flour, spices to mixture and mix well. In a skillet, heat ghee and add ¼ cup of pancake mix at a time (try to cook 2 at a time).
5. Cook until brown color appears and remove from pan. Before serving, top with add little maple syrup, mixed dry cherries and enjoy the taste.

Nutritional Information

- Preparation Time: 20 minutes
- Total servings: 8
- Calories: 233.5 (per serving)
- Fat: 23.5g
- Protein: 7.3g
- Carbs: 3.5g

Recipe 9: Feta Wraps

Ingredients

- Large eggs 2
- Large egg whites 2
- Ghee 2 tsp.
- Black beans 1 oz. (paste)
- Salt ½ tsp.
- Feta cheese 1.5 oz.
- Mascarpone cheese 1 oz.
- Coriander 2 tbsp.
- Sundried tomato 1 (sliced)
- Fresh black pepper flakes 1 tsp.

Preparation Method

1. At first, mix eggs, egg whites, salt, ghee in a mixing bowl until it comes to desired consistency.
2. Place pan over medium heat and make square shaped omelets.
3. Meantime, smash beans and spread over omelet then spread grated cheese, coriander, chopped sundried tomato, sprinkle smashed black pepper flakes and roll the omelet to enjoy delicious taste.

Nutritional Information

- Preparation Time: 15 minutes
- Total servings: 2
- Calories: 366 (per serving)
- Fat: 33.3g
- Protein: 15.8g
- Carbs: 7g

Recipe 10: Fat Rich Broccoli

Ingredients

- Crushed peanuts ½ cup
- Flax seeds 2 oz.
- Chia seeds 2 oz.
- Cauliflower 2 oz.
- Avocado ½ piece
- Coconut milk 3 cups
- Cream ¼ cup
- Cream cheese 2 oz.
- Butter 1 tbsp.
- Ghee 2 tbsp.
- Protein powder 2 tbsp.
- Fruit extract ½ tsp.
- All spice ¼ tsp.
- Erythritol 1 oz

Preparation Method

- Mix flax and chia seeds in small cup and keep aside. In food processor, add broccoli, protein powder and keep aside.
- Toast the raw peanuts in pan (before you toast, smash peanuts into small pieces)
- In another pan, add coconut milk and boil until it cooked well.
- Decrease heat under pan and add allspice, erythritol and stir well.
- Now, add flax seeds and chia seeds to the pan and mix well. When it starts to thicken tremendously.
- Add cream, butter, avocado, ghee, peanuts, and mix together well and make bit thicker and enjoy the taste.

Nutritional Information

- Preparation Time: 15 minutes
- Total servings: 6
- Calories: 477.6 (per serving)
- Fat: 32.3g
- Protein: 12.6g
- Carbs: 4.8g

Recipe 11: Chicken Avocado Rolls

Ingredients

- Bacon 4 slices
- Large eggs 5
- Chicken 2 oz
- Tomato 1
- Avocado 1
- Ghee 1 tbsp.
- Spring onions 1 oz.
- Oregano 2 tbsp.
- Salt and pepper to taste

Preparation Method

1. Dice all vegetables which are listed above.
2. On the other side, fry meat in a pan with ghee and in another pan fry chicken.
3. Once chicken are crispy, add vegetables to the pan and mix together until it mixed well and seasoned as needed.
4. Once spring onions are translucent, add oregano to the pan and mix everything together and add bacon and allow it to cook for 2 minutes.
5. Add eggs and mix everything together and let it cook like an omelet.
6. Before serving, just add avocado paste and roll it to enjoy the delicious taste.

Nutritional Information

- Preparation Time: 25 minutes
- Total servings: 3
- Calories: 469.8 (per serving)
- Fat: 36g
- Protein: 19.1g
- Carbs: 5.3g

Recipe 12: Bacon Coconut Pancakes

Ingredients

Pancake

- Bacon slices 8
- Coconut flour 2 oz.
- Almond flour 6 oz.
- Protein powder 1 tbsp.
- Swerve 2 oz.
- Baking soda ½ tsp.
- Cream of tartar 1 tsp.
- Eggs 4
- Ghee 2 oz.
- Almond milk 16 fl oz.
- Stevia 10 drops

Chocolate dip

- White chocolate 2 oz.
- Ghee 2 tbsp.
- Swerve 2 tbsp.

Preparation Method

1. At first, prepare the crispy bacon by placing in oven (375F) for 15 minutes, until the bacon is browned.
2. For making pancakes, combine all pancakes ingredients into a bowl and mix well.
3. Heat a large pan by adding with ghee, when ghee is hot, pour the batter with regular spoon and top with slice of crispy bacon and cook for 10 minutes each side.
4. Meanwhile, make chocolate dip, mix all ingredients and serve with the pancakes.

Nutritional Information

- Preparation Time: 30 minutes
- Total servings: 2 (4 pancakes per serving)
- Calories: 522 (per serving)
- Fat: 47.4g
- Protein: 21.1g
- Carbs: 5.8g

Recipe 13: Mascarpone Eggs

Ingredients

- Bacon fat 1 tbsp.
- Eggs 2
- Ghee 1 tbsp.
- Mascarpone cheese 2 tbsp.
- Fresh dill 1 tbsp.
- Cilantro 2 tbsp.
- Salt and pepper to taste

Preparation Method

1. Before heating pan, shred the cheese and chop the dill, cilantro.
2. Now, heat the pan with bacon fat in medium low heat, add eggs, cilantro, dill, salt and pepper.
3. Once edges are starting to turn a light brown color, add ghee on top and start smashing until it becomes small pieces.
4. Switch off pan and add cheese on center and start mixing from four sides.
5. Cook until it turns slightly golden color and if desired, enjoy with cooked bacon slices.

Nutritional Information

- Preparation Time: 15 minutes
- Total servings: 1
- Calories: 221 (per serving)
- Fat: 32.5g
- Protein: 16.4g
- Carbs: 3.2g

Recipe 14: Pepper Omelet

Ingredients

- Bacon 2 slices (cooked)
- Bacon fat 1 tbsp.
- Pepper 2 tbsp.
- Large eggs 2
- Ghee 1 tbsp
- Mascarpone cheese 2 tbsp.
- Parmesan cheese 1 tbsp.
- Rosemary 2 stems
- Salt and pepper to taste

Preparation Method

1. Before heating pan, shred the cheese and cooked bacon and chop the thyme
2. Now heat the pan with bacon fat in medium low heat, add eggs, mint, salt and chopped pepper.
3. Once edges are starting to turn a light brown color, add bacon to the center of the pan and cook for 30 seconds by adding ghee on top.
4. Switch off pan and add cheeses on center and start folding from four sides of omelet slowly.
5. Now, turn the omelet and cook until it turns slightly golden color. Enjoy the delicious bacon omelet.

Nutritional Information

- Preparation Time: 15 minutes
- Total servings: 1
- Calories: 579 (per serving)
- Fat: 47.1g
- Protein: 22.9g
- Carbs: 5.3g

Recipe 15: Cabbage Bread

Ingredients

Bread:

- Chia flour 7 oz.
- Pumpkin spice 2 tsp.
- Cream of tartar 1 tsp.
- Baking soda ¼ tsp.
- Lemons zest 1 tbsp.
- Ghee 2 oz.
- Large eggs 4
- Erythritol 3 oz.
- Cinnamon 1 tsp.
- Cabbages puree 5 oz.

Topping:

- Cream cheese 21 oz.
- Small egg 1
- Erythritol 1.5 oz.
- Cinnamon ½ tsp.
- Cabbages puree 3.5 oz.
- Lemons zest 1 tbsp.
- Pinch of salt

Preparation Method

1. At first, preheat your oven to 300F. In a large bowl, add chia flour, cinnamon, pumpkin spice, cream of tartar, baking soda and mix well and add eggs, ghee, Erythritol, cinnamon and mix well.
2. Add a spoon of cabbages puree and mix well (fresh puree gives better taste then canned).
3. Now, add juice and zest half of a lemon and mix. In another bowl, prepare the cheesecake topping by mixing all topping ingredients.
4. Spoon the bread batter into a baking dish suitable for bread and distribute evenly using a ladle. Add a layer using half of the cheese mixture on top of the bread batter and spread evenly.
5. Mix the remaining cheese mixture with the cabbages puree. Gently spoon the cabbage cheese mixture on top and spread evenly. Transfer into the preheated oven and bake for 60 minutes, make sure that bread is not going to burnt on top.
6. Carefully remove from the baking dish, slice into 12 pieces and enjoy the taste.

Nutritional Information

- Preparation Time: 80 minutes
- Total servings: 12
- Calories: 309 (per serving)
- Fat: 30.3g
- Protein: 9.9g
- Carbs: 5.4g

Recipe 16: Arugula Avocado Bowl

Ingredients

- Arugula 1 cup
- Brussels sprouts 1 cup (sautéed)
- Avocado ½ piece (sliced)
- Ghee 1 tbsp.
- Mascarpone cheese 2 oz.
- Red chili sauce 1 tbsp.
- Mint 2 tbsp.
- Sunflower seeds 1 tbsp.
- Salt and Pepper to taste

Preparation Method

1. At first, sauté sprouts for approximately 15 minutes or until lightly browned and tender then slice half avocado.
2. Finally, in a large bowl place arugula, mint, sprouts avocado, mascarpone cheese, sunflower seeds as a layer and enjoy the yummy taste.

Nutritional Information

- Preparation Time: 20 minutes
- Total servings: 2
- Calories: 311 (per serving)
- Fat: 20.6g
- Protein: 10.7g
- Carbs: 5g

Recipe 17: Almond Kimchi Bowl

Ingredients

- Halloumi cheese 2
- Kimchi 2 oz.
- Black sesame seeds 1 tsp.
- Almond flakes 3 tbsp.
- Chili flakes 1 tsp.
- Broccoli 2 tbsp.
- Mascarpone cheese 1 oz.

Sauce:

- Tahini 2 tbsp.
- Lemon juice 3 tbsp.
- Chili sauce 3 tbsp.
- Cayenne pepper 1 tsp.

Preparation Method

1. At first, combine sauce ingredients in a small bowl then stir until smooth and creamy (add more water to thin if desire).
2. Now, place the halloumi cheese, mascarpone and kimchi in bowls then top with sauce, black sesame seeds, almond flakes and chili flakes.
3. Finally, enjoy the yummy bowl with delicious taste.

Nutritional Information

- Preparation Time: 15 minutes
- Total servings: 2
- Calories: 384 (per serving)
- Fat: 39.2g
- Protein: 16.7g
- Carbs: 5.2g

Recipe 18: Grilled Chard

Ingredients

- Chard leaves 30
- Ghee 3 tbsp.
- Vinegar 1 tbsp.
- Fresh thyme 1 tsp.
- Fresh lemon grass 1 tsp.
- Garlic cloves 3
- Macadamia nuts 1 oz.
- Almond flakes 1 oz.
- Parmesan cheese 1 oz.

Preparation Method

1. At first, preheat the oven to 400F. I like 10 chard leaves per person, depending on their size. Cut both ends and peel back the first or second layer of leaves and discard. Leave the chard in a pan with boiling salt water for 2 minutes.
2. Drain well and place in a bowl of ghee, vinegar, chopped lemon grass, thyme and garlic. Spread the chard in a layer in a baking tray, sprinkle nuts, almond flakes and cheese. Bake for 10 minutes until it is caramelized.

Nutritional Information

- Preparation Time: 15 minutes
- Total servings: 3
- Calories: 155 (10 kale leaves per serving)
- Fat: 15.6g
- Protein: 7.1g
- Carbs: 3.3g

Recipe 19: Winter Cheese Sandwich

Ingredients

- Winter squash 35 oz.
- Mozzarella 8 oz.
- Mascarpone cheese 2 oz.
- Ghee 2 tbsp.
- Mint paste 2 tbsp.
- Chili powder 1 tbsp.
- Salt and black pepper to taste
- Fennel powder 1 tbsp.
- Cream ½ cup

Preparation Method

1. At first, preheat oven at 450F. Slice a thin slice each winter squash into 3 pieces and place in a flat frying pan or a baked sheet.
2. Apply ghee to summer squash. Season with salt, pepper and sprinkle chili powder over the sliced squash. Fry until softened and heated by, about 15 minutes.
3. Meanwhile, cut the mozzarella, mascarpone, into six ½-inch thick slices. Using a spatula, sandwich each slice between 2 hot squash halves and apply mint, cream. Before serving, garnish with fennel powder and enjoy the taste.

Nutritional Information

- Preparation Time: 20 minutes
- Total servings: 3 pieces
- Calories: 254 (per serving)
- Fat: 23.7g
- Protein: 10.6g
- Carbs: 5.1g

Recipe 20: Cheesy Kumato Sandwich

Ingredients

- Kumato 2 lb.
- Onions slices 1 oz.
- Ghee 2 tbsp.
- Ginger garlic paste 1 tbsp.
- Salt and black pepper to taste
- Mozzarella 7 oz.
- Mascarpone cheese 3 oz.
- Peanut butter 1 tbsp.
- Fresh rosemary 2 branches

Preparation Method

1. At first, preheat your oven at 450F. Slice the bottom of each kumato so that the kumato sit upright. Halve in each case.
2. Cut the kumatos halves, cut on a foil-filled, flat frying pan or a baked sheet. Apply ghee to kumatos. Season with salt, pepper and sprinkle chopped garlic ginger paste over the tomatoes then fill onions in it.
3. Fry until softened and heated by, about 15 minutes. Meanwhile, cut the mozzarella, mascarpone into slices. Using a spatula, sandwich each slice between 2 hot tomato halves and apply peanut butter (heat melts the cheese slightly).
4. Nourish the kumatos with juices collected in the frying pan and served with the fresh rosemary.

Nutritional Information

- Preparation Time: 20 minutes
- Total servings: 6 pieces
- Calories: 255.8(per serving)
- Fat: 20.5g
- Protein: 10g
- Carbs: 5g

Recipe 21: Forest Mushroom Broccoli Bowl

Ingredients

- Macadamia nuts ½ cup
- Coriander 2 cups
- Ginger paste 2 tsp.
- Lemon juice 2 tbsp.
- Salt and pepper to taste
- Mascarpone cheese 3 oz.
- Forest mushrooms 1 lb.
- Broccoli 2 oz.
- Ghee 1 tbsp.

Preparation Method

1. At first, soak macadamia nuts overnight in water then drain water and add macadamia nuts, coriander, ginger, lemon juice, salt, and pepper to food processor then process until smooth.
2. Now, cook broccoli in small pan over medium heat for 10 minutes and keep aside then place large skillet over medium heat with ghee and add forest mushrooms, season with salt and pepper then cook for 10 minutes, don't forget to stir occasionally until all the water has evaporated and they begin to brown and keep aside.
3. Finally, add broccoli, a quarter of the forest mushrooms, mascarpone and top with a tablespoon of the pesto in bowl and enjoy the delicious taste.

Nutritional Information

- Preparation Time: 35 minutes
- Total servings: 4
- Calories: 381 (per serving)
- Fat: 34.4g
- Protein: 15.3g
- Carbs:7g

Recipe 22: Leafy Nut Fry

Ingredients

- Kale 1 oz.
- Dandelion greens 1 oz.
- Turnip greens 1 oz.
- Collards 1 oz.
- Ghee 2 oz.
- Balsamic vinegar 2 tbsp.
- Ginger paste 2 tsp.
- Mascarpone cheese 2 oz.
- Grated cheddar cheese 2 oz.
- Macadamia nuts 1 oz.
- Pistachio 1 tbsp.
- Salt and pepper to taste

Preparation Method

1. At first, preheat your oven to 350F. Place your all greens in baking tray.
2. In a small bowl, whisk ghee, balsamic vinegar, ginger and apply over greens. Season with salt and pepper to taste.
3. Add crushed nuts then over it add cheese and place in preheated oven for 30 minutes then enjoy the taste.

Nutritional Information

- Preparation Time: 40 minutes
- Total servings: 2
- Calories: 389 (per serving)
- Fat: 38.2g
- Protein: 18.9g
- Carbs: 5.6g

Recipe 23: Grilled Cheesy Kale

Ingredients

- Kale leaves 30
- Ghee 1 tbsp.
- Vinegar 1 tbsp.
- Fresh mint 1 tsp.
- Oregano 2 tsp.
- Garlic cloves 3
- Macadamia nuts 1 oz.
- Sunflower seeds 1 oz.
- Cherry tomatoes 4
- Mascarpone cheese 1 oz.

Preparation Method

1. At first, preheat the oven to 400F. I like 15 kale leaves per person, depending on their size. Cut both ends and peel back the first or second layer of leaves and discard. Leave the kale in a pan with boiling salt water for 2 minutes.
2. Drain well and place in a bowl of ghee, vinegar, chopped oregano, mint and garlic. Spread the kale in a layer in a baking tray, sprinkle nuts, halve grape tomatoes, sunflower seeds and cheese. Bake for 10 minutes until it is caramelized.

Nutritional Information

- Preparation Time: 15 minutes
- Total servings: 2
- Calories: 177 (15 kale leaves per serving)
- Fat: 17.9g
- Protein: 7.3g
- Carbs: 4g

Recipe 24: Mixed Squash Salad

Ingredients

- Fresh tomato 1
- Mixed squash 3 oz. (Butter squash, Acorn, Yellow squash)
- Fresh mozzarella cheese 6 oz.
- Turnip greens 1 tbsp.
- Fresh thyme 1 ½ tbsp.
- Ghee 3 tbsp.
- Mascarpone cheese 2 tbsp.
- Vinegar 1 tbsp.
- Fresh black pepper to taste
- Himalaya salt to taste

Preparation Method

1. In a food processor, put chopped fresh basil, turnip leaves with ghee to make the paste.
2. Slice tomato into 1/4″ slices. You should be able to get at least 6 slices from the tomato and mixed squash.
3. Cut mozzarella, mascarpone into slices. Assemble salad by layering tomato, mozzarella, and paste.
4. Season with salt, pepper, and remaining ghee and enjoy the taste.

Nutritional Information

- Preparation Time: 12 minutes
- Serving per Recipe: 2
- Calories:339 (per serving)
- Fat: 40.1g
- Protein: 15.9g
- Carbs: 6.6g

Recipe 25: Pepperoni Broccoli Rice

Ingredients

- Broccoli rice 1 lb.
- Pepperoni 8.5 oz.
- Jalapeno peppers 3 oz.
- Dry red chili 1
- Fresh turnip greens 2 tbsp.
- Fresh rosemary 1 tbsp.
- Ghee 2 tbsp.
- Salt and pepper to taste

Preparation Method

1. At first, grate broccoli and make rice from it. Keep aside.
2. On other side, slice pepperoni, jalapeno peppers, dry red chili and keep aside.
3. Now, place a large skillet over medium heat and add ghee. When ghee is hot, add peppers, chili, turnip greens and pepperoni. Cook until slightly browned.
4. Add the broccoli rice and cook for 10 minutes, season with salt, pepper. Add finely chopped rosemary and enjoy the taste.

Nutritional Information

- Preparation Time: 20 minutes
- Total servings: 4
- Calories: 379 (per serving)
- Fat: 33g
- Protein: 16.1g
- Carbs: 6.5g

Recipe 26: Green Nut Salad

Ingredients

- Mixed greens 1 oz. (spinach, rapini, collards)
- Fresh herbs 1 oz. (Mint, Marjoram)
- Roasted pine nuts 1 oz.
- Pistachio 2 tbsp.
- Vinaigrette 1 ½ tbsp.
- Parmesan cheese 1 tbsp.
- Mascarpone cheese 1 tbsp.
- Potato slices 2
- Ghee 1 tbsp.
- Salt and pepper to taste

Preparation Method

1. Cook bacon until crisp. Measure your greens, herbs and set in a container that can be shaken.
2. Crumble potato, then add the rest of the ingredients to the greens and shake the container with a lid.
3. Add your seasonings and ghee for better taste and shake once again for proper dressing. Serve and enjoy the taste.

Nutritional Information

- Preparation Time: 10 minutes
- Total servings: 2
- Calories: 341 (per serving)
- Fat: 28.3g
- Protein: 11.2g
- Carbs: 5.2g

Recipe 27: Creamy Goji Berries

Ingredients

- Mascarpone 2 oz.
- Large eggs 2
- Mint 2 tbsp. (chopped)
- Cinnamon ¼ tsp.
- Salt ¼ tsp.
- Ghee 1 tbsp.

Filling

- Cream cheese 4 oz.
- Vanilla extracts ½ tsp.
- Erythritol 2 tbsp.
- Goji berries 2 oz.

Preparation Method

1. In a small bowl, add mascarpone cheese, eggs, mint and mix using hand mixer until it becomes completely smooth.
2. Add cinnamon, salt and combine well. Place a nonstick pan over a medium heat and cook like omelet.
3. Meanwhile, prepare to fill by combining all filling ingredients in a bowl and mix using hand mixer until it becomes creamy paste.
4. When the omelet is cooked, spread filling over omelet and top with goji berries and fold it and enjoy with little cream over it.

Nutritional Information

- Preparation Time: 35 minutes
- Total servings: 2
- Calories: 371 (per serving)
- Fat: 25.9g
- Protein: 13.4g
- Carbs: 6g

Recipe 28: Aspaokes Egg Frittata

Ingredients

- Large eggs 10
- Asparagus 12 pieces
- Artichokes 4 pieces
- Spring onions 0.4 oz.
- Red bell pepper 5 oz.
- Cream 2 fl oz.
- Mascarpone cheese 5oz.
- Bacon 3 oz.
- Fresh parsley 2 tbsp.
- Fresh mint 2 tbsp.
- Ghee 2 tbsp.
- Salt and pepper to taste

Preparation Method

1. At first, preheat your oven to 400F. Before we start cooking, slice asparagus, artichokes by cutting the ends, bell pepper into small stripes, spring onion and keep aside.
2. Place pan over medium heat and add ghee. When ghee is hot add all diced ingredients into pan, salt and cook for 5 minutes and keep aside in baking dish
3. In a small bowl, whisk the eggs, cream, salt, black pepper and keep aside. Crumble the mascarpone cheese all over the vegetables and pour the egg mixture over it and place in preheated oven for 20 minutes just until the top becomes firm.
4. After that lay the bacon all over it and place back in the oven for another 15 minutes. Before serving, add chopped parsley and mint then enjoy the taste.

Nutritional Information

- Preparation Time: 60 minutes
- Total servings: 4
- Calories: 521 (per serving)
- Fat: 40.2g
- Protein: 24.8g
- Carbs: 6g

Recipe 29: Sweet Cheese Duck Salad

Ingredients

- Duck breasts 14 oz.
- Bacon slices 4 oz.
- Dates 2 (chopped)
- Romaine lettuce 1.76 lb.
- Salad Dressing 8 tbsp.
- Mascarpone cheese 4 oz.
- Salt and pepper to taste
- Anchovies 1 oz.

Preparation Method

1. At first, preheat your oven to 375F and bake bacons until it becomes crispy approximately 15 minutes and keep aside.
2. Now, make duck breast fry, by placing in oven to 430F, don't forget to season with salt and pepper. Cook for 15 minutes or until golden color and keep aside.
3. Meanwhile, prepare dressing and other ingredients. Use a peeler to make the mascarpone flakes, dates and place the lettuce in a serving bowl and toss with the dressing.
4. Now, slice the duck breasts into thin strips and place on top of the lettuce. Add the mascarpone flakes and crisped up and crumbled bacon, anchovies and enjoy the taste.

Nutritional Information

- Preparation Time: 45 minutes
- Total servings: 4
- Calories: 666 (per serving)
- Fat: 52.5g
- Protein: 28.6g
- Carbs: 7.1g

Recipe 30: Boiled Avocado Salad

Ingredients

- Large hard boiled eggs 4
- Avocado 150g
- Mayonnaise 1 tbsp.
- Fat yogurt 1 tbsp.
- Salt ½ tsp.
- Ghee 1 tbsp.
- Spring onions 1 tsp.
- Nuts 1 oz. (pistachio, Brazil nuts)
- Mascarpone cheese 1 oz.
- Ground pepper to taste

Preparation Method

1. Combine avocado, mayonnaise, yogurt, salt and pepper. Combine with smashed egg and adjust salt and pepper as needed.
2. Sprinkle smashed nuts, spring onions, ghee, mascarpone cheese and enjoy the taste.

Nutritional Information

- Preparation Time: 10 minutes
- Total servings: 6
- Calories: 249.4 (per serving)
- Fat: 21.6g
- Protein: 9.3g
- Carbs: 4.1g

Recipe 31: Turkey Salad

Ingredients

- Spinach 2 oz.
- Dandelion greens ½ oz.
- Roasted Brazil nuts 1 oz.
- Vinaigrette 4 tsp.
- Grated cheese 1 tbsp.
- Mozzarella cheese 1 oz.
- Turkey slices 2 (each 1 oz.)
- Salt and pepper to taste

Preparation Method

1. Cook turkey until crisp. Measure your greens and set in a container that can be shaken.
2. Crumble bacon, then add the rest of the ingredients to the greens and shake the container with a lid.
3. Add your seasonings for better taste and shake once again for proper dressing.
4. Before serving, add mozzarella balls and enjoy the taste.

Nutritional Information

- Preparation Time: 10 minutes
- Serving per Recipe: 1
- Calories: 553 (per serving)
- Fat: 36.4g
- Protein: 16.6g
- Carbs: 7g

Recipe 32: Crumbled Turnip Eggs Cups

Ingredients

- Ghee 2 tsp.
- Diced shallots 1 oz.
- Turnips greens 3 cups
- Large eggs 4
- Butter 4 tsp.
- Salt and ground pepper to taste
- Blue cheese 1 oz.
- Mascarpone cheese 2 oz.
- Garlic cloves 3
- Grated coconut 1 oz.

Preparation Method

1. Preheat oven to 400F. Easily rinse ramekins with butter. Heat a large pan over medium heat, add ghee, shallots and cook 2 minutes.
2. Add turnips, salt and pepper and boil until the spinach fades for about 3 minutes. Mix in blue cheese, mascarpone and remove from the heat.
3. Divide the faded kale under the oven-proof food and make a fountain in the middle of each. Beat egg into each dish and season with grated coconut, cloves, salt and pepper.
4. Place on the baking sheets and bake until the white is set and the yolks are tight around the edges, but still soft in the middle, about 15 minutes and serve immediately.

Nutritional Information

- Preparation Time: 25 minutes
- Total servings: 4
- Calories: 240 (per serving)
- Fat: 20.9g
- Protein: 11.9g
- Carbs: 6.3g

Recipe 33: Chicken Dill Salad

Ingredients

- Mixed green 2 oz.
- Roasted macadamia nuts 1 oz.
- Vinaigrette 4 tsp.
- Parmesan cheese 1 tbsp.
- Chicken breast 2 slices
- Dill 1 tbsp.
- Salt and pepper (as required)

Preparation Method

1. Cook chicken until crispy. Measure your greens and put in a container that can be shaken.
2. Crumble chicken, then add the rest of the ingredients to the greens and shake the container with a lid.
3. Add your spices for better taste, chopped dill and slate once again for proper dressing. Serve and enjoy the taste.

Nutritional Information

- Preparation Time: 10 minutes
- Total servings: 1
- Calories: 344 (per serving)
- Fat: 30.5g
- Protein: 14.3g
- Carbs: 4.5g

Recipe 34: Turkey Quiche

Ingredients

Crust

- Ground turkey 5 oz.
- Coconut flour 5 oz.
- Chia meal 3 tbsp.
- Large eggs 3
- Salt ½ tsp.

Filling

- Large eggs 6
- Ghee 1 tbsp.
- Heavy whipping cream 4 fl oz.
- Spring onions 1 oz.
- Cheddar cheese 7 oz.
- Mascarpone cheese 4 oz.
- Cream cheese 8 oz.
- Asparagus spears 8 oz.
- Salt and pepper to taste
- Fennel for garnish

Preparation Method

1. At first, preheat the oven to 400F. Put ground turkey into a food processor or blender and make powder.
2. Add powdered rind in a mixing bowl together with the coconut flour and chia meal, Himalaya salt and mix until well combined.
3. Now, crack the eggs and mix the dough using hand or hand mixer, place this dough in a rectangular baking tray with removable bottom (30 x 20 cm / 12 x 8 inch).
4. Bake in preheated oven for 15 minutes and keep aside until it cools down. Reduce the oven to 350F.
5. Now, add shredded cheese's (cheddar and mascarpone) over cooled crust and keep aside. Meantime, take a large bowl and crack the eggs, add the cream, season with salt and pepper and whisk until it combines well
6. On the other hand, place a pan over medium heat with ghee. When ghee is hot, add sliced spring onions and cook for 3 minutes or until fragrant. Add this to the egg mixture and combine well. Add cream cheese to egg mixture and pour over shredded cheese.
7. Now, top egg mixture with asparagus and place in preheated oven for 30 minutes or until lightly browned and crispy on top.
8. Garnish with freshly chopped fennel and enjoy the taste.

Nutritional Information

- Preparation Time: 60 minutes
- Total servings: 8
- Calories: 600 (per serving)
- Fat: 44.1g

- Protein: 24.4g
- Carbs: 6.5g

Recipe 35: Turkey Summer Zoodles

Ingredients

- Turkey breast 3.5 oz.
- Butter 1 tbsp.
- Ghee 1tbsp.
- Curry powder ½ tsp.
- Spring onion 1 stalk
- Garlic 1 clove
- Large egg 1
- Sprouts 1 oz.
- Summer squash 3.5 oz.
- Soy sauce 1 tsp.
- Chili sauce ½ tsp.
- Pepper ¼ tsp.
- Lime juice 1 tsp.
- Toasted white sesame seeds 2 tsp.
- Green chilies 1
- Cilantro 1 tbsp.
- Salt and pepper to taste

Preparation Method

1. At first, season the turkey with curry powder, salt and pepper and keep aside.
2. Prepare the sauce by combining soy sauce, chili sauce.
3. Finely chop spring onion, garlic and make zoodles out of summer squash (use spiralizer)
4. Fry the seasoned turkey with butter until brown.
5. In a pan, melt ghee and chopped spring onion until fragrant and add garlic, egg into the pan.
6. Add sprouts and zoodles and mix everything well together. Add sauce and stir and reduce until there is little liquid left.
7. Add fried chicken pieces and stir and garnish with a few chopped green chilies, cilantro and squeeze some lemon juice on top and sprinkle sesame seeds. Serve and enjoy the taste.

Nutritional Information

- Preparation Time: 20 minutes
- Total servings: 1
- Calories: 599 (per serving)
- Fat: 46.4g
- Protein: 22g
- Carbs: 6.4g

Recipe 36: Chili Turkey Cups

Ingredients

- Lean turkey 2 lb.
- Red pepper 2 oz.
- Broth 1 cup
- Tomato paste 1 oz.
- Light soy sauce 1 ½ tbsp.
- Ghee 1 oz.
- Green chili 1 tbsp. (chopped)
- Fish sauce 1 tsp.
- Ginger garlic paste 2 tsp.
- Cayenne pepper 1 tsp.
- Cheddar cheese 2 oz.
- Coconut milk 2 oz.
- Salt to taste

Preparation Method

1. At first, cut the lean turkey into small cubes. Then cut red pepper into small pieces.
2. In a separate bowl, add broth, tomato paste, light soy sauce, chili, ginger garlic paste, cayenne pepper and mix well.
3. In a pan, heat ghee and add your turkey, continue cooking the turkey until it is browned for 25 minutes, after 10 minutes, add chopped pepper, chopped green chili, coconut milk, salt and seasonings.
4. Cook for 25 minutes and before serving add grated cheddar cheese to enjoy nice taste.

Nutritional Information

- Preparation Time: 60 minutes
- Total servings: 4
- Calories: 343 (per serving)
- Fat: 42.3g
- Protein: 20.8g
- Carbs: 5.7g

Recipe 37: Sesame Layered Turkey Chicken

Ingredients

- Flax meal 1 ¼ cup
- Large eggs 2
- Turkey sausages 2
- Chicken sausages 2
- Vegetable oil 150ml (for frying)
- Heavy cream 1 oz.
- Allspice 1 tsp.
- Salt ½ tsp.
- Chili powder 1 tsp.
- BBQ sauce 2 tbsp.
- Toasted sesame seeds 2 tbsp.

Preparation Method

1. In a mixing bowl, add flax meal, allspice and mix all the dry ingredients well so they are completely distributed.
2. Add your eggs, baking soda and heavy cream to the batter and mix everything well until a nice thick batter is formed.
3. In a saucepan, heat vegetable oil to 400F. Cut each sausage into 2 pieces and mix half turkey and half chicken sausage into single sausage; dip mixed .sausages in the batter before you fry them. Make sure they're fully coated
4. Drop your sausage into the oil 1 at a time. Let it cook for 5 minutes on one side, then flip it and cook for about 2 minutes on the other side.
5. Remove your sausages from the pan and let it dry on some paper towels. Sprinkle toasted sesame seeds over it the dish out with some hot sauces with hot BBQ sauce and enjoy the taste.

Nutritional Information

- Preparation Time: 10 minutes
- Serving per Recipe: 4
- Calories:382.3 (per serving)
- Fat: 36.7g
- Protein: 17g
- Carbs: 5.2g

Recipe 38: Wild Bacon Mushroom

Ingredients

- Egg 1
- Bacon slices 2
- Wild mushrooms 1 oz.
- Sweet potato 2 oz.
- Yellow pepper 1 oz.
- Ghee 2 tbsp.
- Salt and pepper to taste
- Fresh thyme 1 tbsp.

Preparation Method

1. In a small pan, roast the wild mushrooms with ghee and season with salt, pepper. Keep aside.
2. Now, roast the bacon, sweet potato cubes, yellow pepper and keep aside. In the same pan, make an omelet with egg and garnish with freshly chopped thyme.
3. Finally, place all items on serving plate and enjoy the taste.

Nutritional Information

- Preparation Time: 15 minutes
- Total servings: 1
- Calories: 404 (per serving)
- Fat: 36g
- Protein: 15g
- Carbs: 6.1g

Recipe 39: Cheese Cabbage Sausage

Ingredients

- Sausage 1.5 oz.
- Cabbage 2 oz.
- Parmesan cheese 0.5 oz.
- Mascarpone cheese 1 oz.
- Mozzarella 0.5 oz.
- Oregano 1 tsp.
- Basil 1 tsp.
- Salt ½ tsp.
- Coriander paste 1 tsp.
- Red pepper ½ tsp.
- Ghee 2 tbsp.

Preparation Method

1. At first, preheat the oven to 350F. Place the skillet over medium heat and ghee.
2. When ghee is hot, add sausage, cook for 15 minutes and keep aside.
3. Meanwhile, slice cabbage and cook in skillet until it turns to golden brown color
4. Now, cut sausages into round slices and put back in skillet, add Parmesan cheese, mascarpone cheese and stir once.
5. Your skillet into preheated oven for 15 minutes before you remove sprinkle grated mozzarella cheese and chopped herbs. Let it cool for 10 minutes and enjoy the taste.

Nutritional Information

- Preparation Time: 25 minutes
- Total servings: 1
- Calories: 599 (per serving)
- Fat: 47.7g
- Protein: 28.4g
- Carbs: 5.5g

Recipe 40: Cheesy Asparagus Salad

Ingredients

- Asparagus 2 oz. (cooked)
- Pine nuts 1 oz. (roasted)
- Vinaigrette 4 tsp.
- Parmesan cheese 1 tbsp.
- Mascarpone cheese 1 oz.
- Bacon 2 slices
- Salt and pepper to taste

Preparation Method

1. Cook bacon until crisp. Measure your asparagus and set in a container that can be shaken.
2. Crumble bacon, then add the rest of the ingredients to the beans and shake the container with a lid.
3. Add your seasonings for better taste and shake once again for proper dressing.
4. Before serving, add mozzarella balls and enjoy the taste.

Nutritional Information

- Preparation Time: 10 minutes
- Serving per Recipe: 1
- Calories: 534 (per serving)
- Fat: 40.7g
- Protein: 18.1g
- Carbs: 6.2g

Recipe 41: Ghee Rind Balls

Ingredients
Meatballs

- Ghee 1 tbsp.
- Ground rind 0.5 lb.
- Onions 1 oz.
- Garlic cloves 2
- Flax meal 1 oz.
- Coconut milk 1 tbsp.
- Salt to taste

Coconut Broth

- Coconut milk 2 oz.
- Broth 2 oz.

Spices

- Coriander seeds 1 tsp.
- Turmeric ½ tsp.
- Cinnamon ½ tsp.
- Red pepper ½ tsp.
- Ginger powder ½ tsp.
- Garlic powder ½ tsp.
- Chili paste 1 tsp.

Preparation Method

1. In a large pan, add ghee. When ghee is hot, add garlic, onions and cook until fragrant and translucent.
2. Meantime, combine flax meal, coconut milk, ground rind, salt and create a paste.
3. Add onions, garlic to this paste and create small balls using hand. Place the pan over medium heat and add ghee. When ghee is hot add meatballs all over the pan (ca. 15 minutes).
4. When meat are browned on both sides, add coconut milk, broth, and all spices, mix well and cook for 20 more minutes.
5. Finally, serve with some coconut broth with meatballs in a bowl and enjoy the taste.

Nutritional Information

- Preparation Time: 30 minutes
- Total servings: 2
- Calories: 572 (per serving)
- Fat: 46.9g
- Protein: 23.4g
- Carbs: 5.4g

Recipe 42: Vinaigrette Lamb Fry

Ingredients

Lamb Chops

- Lamb chops 4
- Ghee 1 oz.
- Salt and pepper to taste
- Paprika 1 tsp.
- Small better melon 1
- Catnip 1 tsp.

Vinaigrette

- Vinegar 2 tbsp.
- Lemon juice 1 tbsp.
- Maple syrup 1 tbsp.
- Salt and pepper to taste

Topping

- Parsley 1 tbsp.

Preparation Method

1. At first, season lamb chops with salt, pepper, ghee and keep aside.
2. Place large iron skillet over high heat and add seasoned lamb chops and cook 10 minutes both side.
3. Decrease the heat to medium and add better melon slices, catnip over the lamb chops and place in the oven for about 10 minutes at 350F.
4. Meanwhile, prepare vinaigrette by mixing all the ingredients together. When lamb chops are ready, pour vinaigrette over top then sprinkle parsley and serve hot.

Nutritional Information

- Preparation Time: 25 minutes
- Total servings: 2
- Calories: 488 (per serving)
- Fat: 40.7g
- Protein: 21.3g
- Carbs: 5.3g

Recipe 43: Bacon Cheese Layer

Ingredients

- Bacon 4 oz.
- Mozzarella cheese 5 oz.
- Cheddar cheese 3.5 oz.
- Mascarpone cheese 3 oz.
- Coconut flour 4 tbsp.
- Chia meal 3 tbsp.
- Egg yolk 1
- Herb seasoning 1 tsp.
- Salt and pepper to taste

Preparation Method

1. At first, preheat the oven to 400F and in a microwave or toaster oven, melt your mozzarella cheese. About 1 minute in the microwave, and 10 second intervals afterward, or about 10 minutes in an oven, stirring occasionally.
2. In a mixing bowl, mix chia meal, herb seasonings, salt, pepper, mozzarella (melted), mascarpone, egg yolk and make moist dough, transfer it to a flat surface with some parchment paper.
3. Using rolling pin flatten dough and using knife cut diagonal lines beginning from the edges of the dough to the center, leave a row of dough untouched about 4 inches wide.
4. Alternate lay bacon slices and cheddar on that uncut stretch of dough then cover your filling by lift one section of dough at a time and lay it over the top.
5. Finally, bake in preheated oven for 20 minutes until you see it has turned a golden brown color and enjoy the taste.

Nutritional Information

- Preparation Time: 40 minutes
- Total servings: 4
- Calories: 343 (per serving)
- Fat: 37.4g
- Protein: 24.2g
- Carbs: 5.4g

Recipe 44: Cabbage Cheese Meal

Ingredients

- Ghee 1 tbsp.
- Egg 1
- Cream cheese 1 tbsp.
- Mozzarella 1 tbsp.
- Mascarpone cheese 1tbsp.
- Flax flour 2 tbsp.
- Chia meal 1 tbsp.
- Baking soda ½ tsp.
- Salt to taste

Filling

- Cabbage 2 oz.
- Bacon slices 2
- Roasted garlic cloves 3

Toppings

- Mayonnaise 2 tbsp.
- Vinegar 1 tsp.
- BBQ sauce 1 tbsp.
- Sage 1 tbsp.

Preparation Method

1. In a small bowl mix mayonnaise, rice vinegar and keep aside. In a mixing bowl, add ghee, cream cheese, mascarpone, mozzarella and mix until softened.
2. Now, add almond flour, chia meal, baking soda, salt to the mixing bowl and mix well. Now, add egg into the batter, add cabbage and stir until fully incorporated.
3. Place large skillet over medium heat and add sliced bacon until it becomes crispy.
4. Spread incorporated batter into bacon skillet and cook for 5 minutes or until batter turns to golden color on the bottom.
5. Flip and cook again 5 minutes and transfer to a plate. Spread BBQ sauce, mayonnaise, vinegar and roasted garlic.
6. Finally, sprinkle sage and enjoy the taste.

Nutritional Information

- Preparation Time: 30 minutes
- Total servings: 2
- Calories: 498 (per serving)
- Fat: 46.2g
- Protein: 12.5g
- Carbs: 5.2g

Recipe 45: Summer Bacon Fry

Ingredients

- Summer squash 7 oz.
- Bacon 2 oz.
- Onions 1 oz.
- Garlic clove 2
- Ghee 1 tbsp.
- Fresh parsley 1 tbsp.
- Salt ¼ tsp.

Preparation Method

1. At first, chop onions, garlic, bacon and add it to large skillet over a medium heat and cook until it turns light brown color.
2. On the other hand, dice the summer squash into medium cube size pieces and add to skillet, cook for 15 minutes. Don't forget to stir frequently and finally add chopped parsley.

Nutritional Information

- Preparation Time: 25 minutes
- Total servings: 1
- Calories: 411 (per serving)
- Fat: 34.1g
- Protein: 17g
- Carbs: 6.2g

Recipe 46: Coriander Bacon

Ingredients

- Bacon 4 slices
- Eggs 5
- Pork 2 oz. (boneless)
- Tomato slices 3
- Avocado 1
- Onion 1 oz.
- Ghee 1 tbsp.
- Coriander paste 1 tbsp.
- Salt and pepper to taste

Preparation Method

1. At first, fry pork in ghee, once pork is crispy, add tomato sauce to the skillet and mix until blended well and season with salt and pepper as needed.
2. Add onions, coriander paste in the pan and mix everything together and add bacon and let it boil for 2 minutes.
3. Add eggs and mix everything together and let it boil like an omelet. Before serving, just add avocado cubes and mix. Enjoy the delicious taste.

Nutritional Information

- Preparation Time: 25 minutes
- Total servings: 3
- Calories: 488 (per serving)
- Fat: 40.1g
- Protein: 20.4g
- Carbs: 5.2g

Recipe 47: Fennel Lamb

Ingredients

- Fennel 8 oz.
- Ghee 1 tbsp.
- Mascarpone cheese 2 oz.
- Mozzarella cheese 1 oz.
- Coconut cream 2 oz.
- Ground lamb 2 oz.
- Thyme 2 tbsp.
- Salt and black pepper to taste

Preparation Method

1. At first, in large e skillet, add half ghee. When ghee is hot, add ground lamb and cook for 15 minutes
2. Meantime, remove middle flesh of fennel and lace in baking tray with the remaining ghee and salt and pepper.
3. Add cooked meat. Layer cheese and coconut cream as topping and shake the fennel occasionally, cook until it is tender and slightly charred in oven for minimum 20 minutes. Before serving sprinkle thyme and enjoy the taste.

Nutritional Information

- Preparation Time: 40 minutes
- Total servings: 2
- Calories: 221.2 (per serving)
- Fat: 23.2g
- Protein: 11.8g
- Carbs: 5.4g

Recipe 48: Rind Squash Rolls

Ingredients
Filling:

- Rind 4 oz.
- Celery 1 stalk
- Medium squash 1
- Ginger ½ tsp.
- Garlic ½ tsp.
- Maple syrup 1 tsp.
- Mascarpone cheese 2 oz.
- Stock powder 1 tsp.

Wrappers:

- Beaten egg 1
- Cornstarch 1 tsp.
- Spring roll wrappers 8
- Ghee 2 tsp.

Preparation Method
1. Filling: In a mixing bowl, add shredded rind, celery, squash, ginger, garlic, maple, stock powder, mascarpone and mix well until it mixes well.
2. On the other side, make a thick paste by mixing egg with the cornstarch and keep aside, then put some filling on each spring roll wrapper and slowly roll.
3. Roll it up with wet hands and seal the ends with the egg mixture.
4. Finally, preheat the oven to 390°F (198°C) and brush the spring rolls with little ghee and place on baking basket then cook for 10 minutes or until it turns to golden brown color.
5. If desired, serve with sweet chili sauce or Sriracha sauce to enjoy better taste.

Nutritional Information
- Preparation Time: 20 minutes
- Total servings: 4
- Calories: 377 (per serving)
- Fat: 24.7g
- Protein: 12.2g
- Carbs: 5g

Recipe 49: Layered Asparagus Lamb

Ingredients

- Asparagus 0.5 lb. (trimmed)
- Ghee 2 tbsp.
- Mascarpone cheese 2 oz.
- Parmesan cheese 1 oz.
- Coconut cream 2 oz.
- Lamb 3 oz.
- Salt and black pepper to taste

Preparation Method

1. At first, in large e skillet, add ghee. When ghee is hot, add chopped lamb and cook for 20 minutes.
2. In baking tray, dice the asparagus with the remaining ghee and salt and pepper.
3. Brush the asparagus in a single layer and add cooked lamb. Layer cheese and coconut cream as topping and shake the baking tray occasionally, until it is tender and slightly charred, 15 minutes.

Nutritional Information

- Preparation Time: 40 minutes
- Total servings: 2
- Calories: 248.9 (per serving)
- Fat: 23.6g
- Protein: 8.9g
- Carbs: 4.3g

Recipe 50: Rindfleisch Casserole

Ingredients

- Hackfleisch (rind) 1 lb.
- Spring onions 3 oz.
- Ginger paste 1 tbsp.
- Mustard powder1 tbsp.
- Cheddar cheese 6 oz.
- Mascarpone cheese 2 oz.
- Large eggs 6
- Heavy whipping cream 4 fl oz.
- Ghee 4 tbsp.
- Salt and pepper to taste

Preparation Method

1. At first, preheat your oven to 350F. Place large pan over medium heat and add ghee. When ghee is hot, add ground rind and break all large pieces.
2. Cook until the meat is browned from all sides, about 15 minutes and add to the large mixing bowl and keep aside.
3. Now, slice spring onions, ginger paste and cook in the same pan which is used to cook rind until fragrant and lightly browned, about 10 minutes.
4. Add shredded cheddar cheese, mascarpone and mix until well combined (save little cheese for topping purpose).
5. Crack the eggs in a small bowl and mix with the cream, salt, pepper and pour in mixing bowl. Top with the remaining cheddar cheese and place in preheated oven for 25 minutes or until the top is golden brown. Just before serving, add hot sauce on top and enjoy the taste.

Nutritional Information

- Preparation Time: 50 minutes
- Total servings: 4
- Calories: 581 (per serving)
- Fat: 49g
- Protein: 28.8g
- Carbs: 6.7g

Recipe 51: Mascarpone Salmon Wraps

Ingredients

- Large eggs 3
- Avocado 3.5 oz.
- Smoked salmon 2 oz.
- Mascarpone cheese 2 tbsp.
- Fresh dill 2 tbsp.
- Cabbage 4 tbsp.
- Ghee 1 tbsp.
- Salt and pepper to taste

Preparation Method

1. At first, whisk egg, salt and pepper in a small bowl, add mascarpone cheese with chopped dill and keep aside.
2. Place pan over medium heat and add ghee, cabbage. When ghee is hot, add egg mixture into pan and cook for 1 minute each side.
3. Meanwhile, slice the smoked salmon, avocado and keep aside. Now, place the omelet on a plate and add sliced salmon, avocado and fold into a wrap.

Nutritional Information

- Preparation Time: 15 minutes
- Total servings: 2
- Calories: 388.7 (per serving)
- Fat: 34.6g
- Protein: 16.6g
- Carbs: 4.2g

Recipe 52: Smoked Salmon Salad

Ingredients

- Smoked salmon 1 lb.
- Dark soy sauce 1 tbsp.
- Ghee 1 tbsp.
- Water 1 tbsp.
- Garlic paste 1 tsp.
- Mascarpone cheese 2 oz.
- Vinegar 2 tsp.
- Lemon juice 1 tbsp.
- Chopped parsley 1 tbsp.
- Baby chard 1 oz.

Preparation Method

1. At first, cut the smoked salmon and set aside and work on the marinating. Combine all ingredients such as soy sauce, ghee, water, garlic paste and vinegar.
2. Mix the ham and marinade mixture in a bowl and keep aside for 30 minutes. Preheat oven to 350F, place ham on a baking tray covered with parchment paper and bake for 30 minutes.
3. Once smoked salmon is ready, sprinkle parsley, baby chard, lemon juice and enjoy the taste.

Nutritional Information

- Preparation Time: 65 minutes
- Total servings: 3
- Calories: 444.3 (per serving)
- Fat: 36g
- Protein: 17.2g
- Carbs: 5.9g

Recipe 53: Marjoram Salmon

Ingredients

- Salmon fillets 1 lb.
- Marjoram paste 3 tbsp.
- Macadamia nuts 1 oz.
- Maple syrup 1 tbsp.
- Mustard ½ tsp.
- Dill ¼ tsp.
- Ghee 1 tbsp.
- Salt and pepper to taste

Preparation Method

1. Preheat the oven to 350F. Add macadamia nuts, marjoram, maple syrup, your spices and mustard in food processor and make a paste.
2. Heat the pan and add ghee and fry dry salmon fillets for about 3 minutes. Add the paste to the top side of salmon fillets.
3. Once they seared, transfer them to an oven and bake for about 10 minutes. Serve with some fresh baby spinach and smoked paprika to enjoy extra taste.

Nutritional Information

- Preparation Time: 15 minutes
- Serving per Recipe: 2
- Calories: 391 (per serving)
- Fat: 42.1g
- Protein: 18.8g
- Carbohydrates: 5.2g

Recipe 54: Pistachio Tuna

Ingredients
- Pistachio 1 oz.
- Maple syrup 1 tbsp.
- Tuna fillets 1 lb.
- Ghee 2 tbsp.
- All-spice 1 tsp.
- Tarragon 2 tsp.
- Salt and pepper to taste

Preparation Method
1. At first, preheat your oven to 350F. Add pistachio, maple syrup, all-spices and, tarragon in the blender and make a paste.
2. Heat the pan and add ghee and fry tuna fillets for about 5 minutes. Add the pistachio paste to the top of the tuna fillets.
3. Once fried, transfer them to an oven and bake for about 5 minutes. Serve with a little fresh baby spinach and a little paprika. Enjoy the delicious taste.

Nutritional Information
- Preparation Time: 15 minutes
- Total servings: 2
- Calories: 357 (per serving)
- Fat: 42g
- Protein: 18.8g
- Carbs: 4.8g

Recipe 55: Smoked Spring Frittata

Ingredients

- Ghee 2 tbsp.
- Spring onions ¼ cup
- Large eggs 6
- Cream 2 tbsp.
- Hot sauce ½ tbsp.
- Smoked trout fillets 2
- Mascarpone cheese 2 oz.
- Fresh rosemary (handful)

Preparation Method

1. At first, heat ghee in a frying pan, and then cook the spring onions until softened.
2. Preheat your oven to 160C.
3. In a small bowl, whisk the eggs, sour cream, mascarpone and horseradish sauce then tip the onions into a cooking basket.
4. Cook for 20 minutes or until the frittata is turn to golden color and sprinkle chopped rosemary.

Nutritional Information

- Preparation Time: 25 minutes
- Total servings: 2
- Calories: 314 (per serving)
- Fat: 23.8g
- Protein: 14g
- Carbs:4.8g

Recipe 56: Roasted Walnut Tuna Filet

Ingredients

- Walnut 1 oz.
- Tuna fillet 1 lb.
- Halloumi cheese 2 oz. (grilled)
- Maple syrup 2 tbsp.
- Roasted mustard seeds ½ tsp.
- Thyme 1 tsp.
- Ghee 2 tbsp.
- Baby spinach 1 cup (steamed)
- Salt and pepper to taste

Preparation Method

1. At first, preheat your oven to 350F. Add walnuts, maple syrup, your spices and mustard in the mixer and make a paste.
2. Rub tuna with ghee and add the walnut paste to the top of the tuna fillets.
3. Transfer them to an oven cooking basket and bake for about 15 minutes. Serve with a little fresh baby spinach, halloumi cheese and a little smoked paprika. Enjoy the delicious taste.

Nutritional Information

- Preparation Time: 25 minutes
- Total servings: 2
- Calories: 364 (per serving)
- Fat: 22.4g
- Protein: 12g
- Carbs: 4.9g

Recipe 57: Grilled Mascarpone Salmon

Ingredients

- Smoked salmon1 lb.
- Mascarpone cheese 2oz.
- Ghee 2 tbsp.
- Asparagus ½ stem
- Vinegar 2 tbsp.
- Thyme ½ tsp.
- Lavender ½ tsp.
- Basil ½ tsp.
- Thyme ½ tsp.
- Sea salt to taste

Preparation Method

1. At first, preheat your grill. Whisk ghee, vinegar, and herbs together.
2. Now, mix smoked salmon in herb mixture, it should cover both sides. Lay the smoked salmon on your preheated grill and cook for about 5 minutes on both sides.
3. Finally, add mascarpone cheese on top and grill for 1 minute or until cheese starts to melt then sprinkle sea salt and enjoy the taste.

Nutritional Information

- Preparation Time: 10 minutes
- Total servings: 4
- Calories: 171 (per serving)
- Fat: 13.2g
- Protein: 6.2g
- Carbs: 3.1g

Recipe 58: Squash Tuna Medley

Ingredients

- Ghee 2 tbsp.
- Tuna 4 oz.
- Halloumi cheese 2 oz.
- Summer squash 1 oz.
- Bell pepper 1 oz.
- Soy sauce 4 tbsp.
- Avocado oil 2 tbsp.
- Rapini 2 oz.
- Salt and pepper to taste

Preparation Method

1. At first, place a pan over medium heat and sauté tuna cubes in ghee for 5 minutes or until lite brown color.
2. Add in the squash, peppers, and sauté for 5 minutes then add soy sauce and avocado oil, let the tuna soak in the soy and sesame for 3 minutes.
3. Make and add rapini, halloumi cheese and mix well, don't forget to stir occasionally.
4. If desired, add season with more salt and pepper depending on your taste.

Nutritional Information

- Preparation Time: 15 minutes
- Total servings: 3
- Calories: 351 (per serving)
- Fat: 30.2g
- Protein: 14.9g
- Carbs: 5.1g

Recipe 59: Brazil Sea Bass

Ingredients

- Fresh whole sea bass 1
- Fresh parsley 3 tbsp.
- Fresh mint 3 tbsp.
- Ghee 2 tbsp.
- Broccoli 1 cup
- Mascarpone cheese 2oz. (crumbled)
- Brazil nuts 3 tbsp.
- Lemons juice 2 tbsp.
- Salt and pepper to taste

Preparation Method

1. At first, preheat your oven to 400F then chop the parsley and mint.
2. Now, Place sea bass over baking parchment then rub with ghee then season with salt and pepper. Sprinkle lemon juice and little herbs and bake for 15 minutes or until the thickest part of the fish are cooked.
3. Meanwhile, crumble mascarpone cheese, Brazil nuts. In a bowl mix grated broccoli, herbs, macadamia, lemon juice and 2 tablespoons of ghee then season with salt and pepper to taste.
4. Remove the sea bass from your oven then serve with the broccoli cheese mix salad.

Nutritional Information

- Preparation Time: 20 minutes
- Total servings: 2
- Calories: 419 (per serving)
- Fat: 39g
- Protein: 23g
- Carbs: 5.2g

Recipe 60: Bacon Broccoli Soup

Ingredients

- Vegetable broth 1 ½ cups
- Bacon 4 slices
- Broccoli puree 1 cup
- Ghee 1 oz.
- Butter 1 oz.
- Garlic 1 tsp.
- Ginger 1 tsp.
- Salt ½ tsp.
- Pepper ½ tsp.
- Red chili flakes 2
- Fresh ginger ½ tsp.
- Mint ¼ tsp.
- Bay leaf 1
- Mascarpone cheese 1 oz.

Preparation Method

1. Keep saucepan over medium heat, add ghee. When ghee is hot, add garlic and fresh ginger.
2. Let this sauté for about 3 minutes or until onions start to go translucent then add spices (salt, pepper, coriander, bay leaf, red chili flakes) to the pan and let cook for 2 minutes. Add broccoli puree to pan and stir into the onions and spices well
3. Once the broccoli is mixed well, add vegetable broth to the pan. Stir until everything is combined.
4. Bring to a boil to simmer for 20 minutes. Once simmered, use an immersion blender to blend together all of the ingredients. You want a smooth puree here so make sure you take your time. Cook for an additional 20 minutes.
5. In the meantime, cook 4 slices of bacon over medium heat. Once the soup is ready, pour mascarpone cheese and the grease from the cooked bacon and mix well.
6. Crumble the bacon over the top of the soup and enjoy the taste of the soup.

Nutritional Information

- Preparation Time: 45 minutes
- Serving per Recipe: 3
- Calories:491 (per serving)
- Fat: 45.1g
- Protein: 10.8g
- Carbs: 5.7g

Recipe 61: Soy Lamb Soup

Ingredients

- Lamb bone 1 lb.
- Onion Powder 1 tsp.
- Garlic Powder 1 tsp.
- Ginger powder 1 tsp.
- Chili powder ½ tsp.
- Ghee 2 oz.
- Soy sauce 2 oz.
- Broth 3 cups
- Cream cheese 2 oz.
- Cumin powder 1 tsp.
- Salt and Pepper to taste

Preparation Method

1. Cut or slice the lamb bones into chunks and drop them in the pot and add all the rest of the ingredients to the cooking pot except cream, cheese.
2. Set cooking pot on heat for 60 minutes and cooks completely. Once everything is cooked, remove the lamb from the cooking pot and shred using a fork.
3. Add cream and cheese to the cooking pot. Using an immersion blender, emulsify all of the liquids together. This will help the soup from separating while you are eating.
4. Place the lamb back into the cooking pot, stir together. Taste and season with extra salt, pepper, cumin and soy sauce. Serve and enjoy the taste.

Nutritional Information

- Preparation Time: 190 minutes
- Serving per Recipe: 5
- Calories:531.2 (per serving)
- Fat: 46.3g
- Protein: 22.1g
- Carbs: 5.4g

Recipe 62: Lamb Sausage Soup

Ingredients

- Ground lamb 1 lb.
- Sausage 7 oz.
- Fresh tomatoes 7 oz.
- Tomato Puree 2 oz.
- Onions 2 oz.
- Garlic 3 cloves
- Ginger powder ½ tsp.
- Ghee 4 tbsp.
- Salt and pepper to taste
- Broth 1 liter
- Garnish with sweet marjoram

Preparation Method

1. At first, dice the onion, sausage, tomatoes and keep aside.
2. Place large Dutch pan over medium heat with ghee. Once ghee hot, add the diced onion, garlic, ginger and cook 2 minutes or until lightly browned, cook for 5 minutes, don't forget to stir to prevent burning.
3. Add the sausage, ground lamb into the pot and cook until it turns to brown color. Add the chopped tomatoes, tomato puree.
4. Now, add broth (your choice) and season with salt and pepper. Cook the soup until bubbles appears and before serving, add chopped sweet marjoram for extra flavor.

Nutritional Information

- Preparation Time: 30 minutes
- Total servings: 5
- Calories: 371 (per serving)
- Fat: 32g
- Protein: 15.3g
- Carbs: 6.1g

Recipe 63: Red Chard Cheese Soup

Ingredients

- Ghee 1 tbsp.
- Onion 1 oz.
- Red chard 10 oz.
- Large eggs 8
- Goat cheese 8 oz.
- Mascarpone cheese 2 oz.
- Sea salt 1 tsp.
- Black pepper ½ tsp.

Preparation Method

1. At first, preheat your oven to 350F and place your pan over medium heat. When ghee is hot, add onions and cook until it becomes soft.
2. Add chopped chard and cook for 2 minutes and keep aside. In a bowl, mix egg, goat cheese, mascarpone, salt, pepper and add to mixture.
3. Using blender, blend the mixture and pour into pan, place in preheated oven for 30 minutes and enjoy the taste.

Nutritional Information

- Preparation Time: 40 minutes
- Total servings: 4
- Calories: 580 (per serving)
- Fat: 48g
- Protein: 27.1g
- Carbs: 6.9g

Recipe 64: Turkey Ghee Soup

Ingredients

- Turkey leg 2 lb.
- Broth 240 ml
- Tomatoes 1 oz.
- Cream 1 oz.
- Ghee 1 oz.
- Garlic paste 1 tsp.
- Ginger paste 1 tsp.
- Chili powder 1 tsp.
- Mascarpone 1 oz.
- Sesame seeds 1 tsp. (toasted)
- Salt and pepper to taste
- Thyme 1 tsp.

Preparation Method

1. At first, preheat the oven to 375F, add ghee to the turkey, salt, pepper and place the marinated turkey in the oven for 25 minutes.
2. Cut mascarpone into small cubes pieces and set aside and heat the pan over medium heat and add ghee. When the ghee starts to brown, add ginger, garlic and mix for 2 minutes.
3. Add tomato, sesame seeds, chili powder and salt. Mix well all together. Add broth and let it simmer for 10 minutes and add cream, slowly stir in the medium heat.
4. Add turkey legs pieces gently into the sauce and let it boil for 5 minutes. Garnish with dill and enjoy the taste.

Nutritional Information

- Preparation Time: 35 minutes
- Total servings: 4
- Calories: 482 (per serving)
- Fat: 43g
- Protein: 16.1g
- Carbs: 4.4g

Recipe 65: Savory Beef Soup

Ingredients

- Beef sausage 2 lb.
- Broth 3 cups
- Ghee 2 tsp.
- Rapini 2 oz.
- Onion Powder 1 tsp.
- Chili powder 1 tsp.
- Cumin seeds 1 tsp.
- Garlic Powder 1 tsp.
- Salt ½ tsp.
- Tomatoes 2 oz.
- Savory 1 tbsp.
- Mascarpone cheese 2 oz.

Preparation Method

1. Heat ghee in a large pot over medium heat. Once hot, add sausage to the pan, allow it to cook slightly.
2. As the sausage cooks, season with salt and pepper. Add the tomatoes and stir. Then, add the rapini on top of everything and place the lid on the pot.
3. Cook until rapini is wilted, about 5 minutes. In the meantime, measure out all spices and grab your beef stock to have handy.
4. Once the rapini is wilted, mix it together with the sausage then add the spices and mix again. Lastly, add the broth and mix once again.
5. Reduce the heat to medium and cook for 30 minutes. Reduce the heat to simmer and cook 15 more minutes. Before serving, add mascarpone, savory and enjoy the flavor.

Nutritional Information

- Preparation Time: 55 minutes
- Serving per Recipe: 6
- Calories:474 (per serving)
- Fat: 40.8g
- Protein: 19.9g
- Carbs: 5g

Recipe 66: Pepper Turkey Soup

Ingredients

- Ghee 2 tbsp.
- Turkey breast 1lb.
- Red pepper 3 oz.
- Turkey broth 1 cup
- Water 1 cup
- Cream 4 fl oz.
- Mascarpone cheese 4 oz.
- Brazil nuts powder 1 oz.
- Lemon juice 3 tbsp.
- Large eggs 3
- Salt and pepper to taste

Preparation Method

1. At first, place a large pan over medium heat with ghee. When ghee is hot, add turkey and cook until it turns light brown color.
2. Add your turkey broth, green pepper, water, cream, lemon juice and cook for 10 minutes to allow the pepper to become tender.
3. Meanwhile, beat 3 eggs together in a small bowl and slowly add to the soup and decrease the heat to low and cook for 10 minutes.
4. Now, add shredded mascarpone cheese and nut powder and stir for a few minutes. Turn off heat and serve immediately with some freshly chopped herbs.

Nutritional Information

- Preparation Time: 30 minutes
- Total servings: 4
- Calories: 333 (per serving)
- Fat: 28.8g
- Protein: 15.8g
- Carbs: 5.4g

Recipe 67: Creamy Veggie Soup

Ingredients

- Vegetable broth 1 ½ cup
- Mixed vegetable 1 oz. (eggplant, squash)
- Bouillon 2
- Mascarpone cream 2 tbsp.
- Ghee 1 tbsp.
- Large eggs 2 (boiled)
- Thyme 2 tbsp.
- Chili paste ½ tsp.
- Garlic paste ½ tsp.

Preparation Method

1. Place a pan over medium heat and add vegetable broth, vegetables, bouillon cube, and ghee.
2. Bring the broth to a boil and stir everything together then, add the chili paste, garlic paste and stir again. Turn the stove off.
3. Halve the boiled eggs then add to steaming broth, mascarpone cheese then stir together well and let sit for a moment and add chopped thyme leaves. Serve up some awesome tasting soup in 5 minutes.

Nutritional Information

- Preparation Time: 5 minutes
- Serving per Recipe: 1
- Calories:301 (per serving)
- Fat: 27g
- Protein: 12g
- Carbs: 4.6g

Recipe 68: Red Beefy Soup

Ingredients

- Beef 1 lb.
- Sausage 7 oz.
- Tomatoes 14 oz.
- Herb paste 2 tbsp.
- Red curry paste 1 tbsp.
- Ghee 4 tbsp.
- Broth 1 liter
- Salt and pepper to taste

Garnish

- Fresh parsley 1 tbsp.
- Dill 2 tsp.

Preparation Method

1. At first, dice sausage, tomatoes and keep aside. Place large Dutch pan over medium heat with ghee.
2. Once ghee hot, add red curry paste and cook for 2 minutes or until lightly browned, then don't forget to stir to prevent burning.
3. Add the sausage, beef into the pot and cook until it turns to brown color. Add the chopped tomatoes, broth and season with salt and pepper.
4. Cook the soup until bubbles appears and before serving, adds chopped parsley and dill.

Nutritional Information

- Preparation Time: 30 minutes
- Total servings: 4
- Calories: 3661 (per serving)
- Fat: 29.2g
- Protein: 18g
- Carbs: 6.2g

Recipe 69: Wild Salmon Soup

Ingredients

- Ghee 2 tbsp.
- Bacon 8 oz.
- Wild salmon 3 oz.
- Cauliflower 2 oz.
- Red onions 2 oz.
- Whipping cream 2 oz.
- Mascarpone cheese 2 oz.
- Salt and pepper to taste

Preparation Method

1. At first, place a large saucepan over medium heat and add ghee. When ghee is hot, add bacon, wild salmon and cook for 10 minutes or until crisped up and keep aside.
2. Meanwhile, slice the cauliflower, red onions and cook for another 10 minutes or until it looks tender.
3. Finally, season with salt, pepper, cream, mascarpone and freshly chopped herbs. If desire, before serving add little ghee and enjoy the taste.

Nutritional Information

- Preparation Time: 30 minutes
- Total servings: 4
- Calories: 329 (per serving)
- Fat: 28.9g
- Protein:13.2g
- Carbs: 5.6g

Recipe 70: Cabbage Cheddar Soup

Ingredients

- Ghee 1 tbsp.
- Garlic cloves 2
- Heavy cream 4 oz.
- Vegetable broth 1 cup
- Water 1 cup
- Purple cabbage 4 oz.
- Cheddar cheese 4 oz.
- Macadamia nut powder 2 tbsp.
- Coconut milk 2 tbsp.
- Blue cheese 2 tbsp.
- Salt and pepper to taste
- Paprika 1 tsp.

Preparation Method

1. Place a large soup pot over medium heat and add ghee. When ghee is hot add chopped garlic and cook until translucent.
2. Now, add cream, broth, water and boil for 15 minutes. Season with salt, pepper, and paprika.
3. Meanwhile, cut cabbage into small florets and add to soup, reduce the heat to low and cook for 20 minutes.
4. Once the cabbage is cooked, add shredded cheese's, coconut milk and turn off the heat and serve in serving bowl and sprinkle macadamia nut powder then mix well.

Nutritional Information

- Preparation Time: 45 minutes
- Total servings: 2
- Calories: 361 (per serving)
- Fat: 24.2g
- Protein: 12.7g
- Carbs: 5.2g

Recipe 71: Rind Spring Soup

Ingredients

- Rind cubes 4 oz.
- Spring onions 3 oz.
- Garlic cloves 4
- Ginger 1 tsp.
- Tomatoes 14 oz.
- Coriander powder 2 tsp.
- BBQ Sauce 6 oz.
- Mascarpone cheese 5 oz.
- Ghee 2 oz.
- Rind stock 2 cups
- Salt and pepper to taste
- Water 2 cups

Preparation Method

1. At first, boil the rind for 60 minutes in water, after cooking rind and keep aside.
2. Place large pan over medium heat with ghee. When ghee is hot, add sliced spring onions, garlic, ginger and cook until lightly browned and fragrant. Add rind stock and bring to a boil over a high heat for 15 minutes
3. Meanwhile, cut and add tomatoes then cook another 15 minutes. Now, add BBQ sauce and rind and turn off the heat. Season with coriander powder, salt and pepper.
4. Grate the mascarpone cheese and chopped herbs over soup and serve warm to enjoy the delicious taste.

Nutritional Information

- Preparation Time: 90 minutes
- Total servings: 8
- Calories: 522 (per serving)
- Fat: 39.9g
- Protein: 22g
- Carbs: 6.7g

Recipe 72: Coconut Pork Stew

Ingredients
- Pork 1 lb.
- Ghee 1 oz.
- Onion powder 1 tbsp.
- Garlic powder 2 tsp.
- Ginger powder 1 tsp.
- All spice 1 tsp.
- Salt to taste
- Diced tomatoes 2 oz.
- Coconut milk 4 oz.
- Parsley 1 tbsp.

Preparation Method
1. Cut the pork into small cube size pieces and season with salt, pepper and ground pepper, ginger, garlic and mix well.
2. Add tomatoes and mix well. Finally, add coconut milk and mix.
3. Cook for 40 minutes on medium heat and mix thoroughly then sprinkle chopped parsley. Serve over cauliflower rice or normal rice for nice taste.

Nutritional Information
- Preparation Time: 45 minutes
- Total servings: 5
- Calories: 501 (per serving)
- Fat: 40.8g
- Protein: 25.5g
- Carbs:5g

Recipe 73: Coconut Turkey Stew

Ingredients

- Onions 2 oz.
- Garlic powder 1 tsp.
- Ginger powder 1 tsp.
- Ghee 2 tsp.
- Turkey 1 lb.
- Coconut milk 1 cup
- Parsley 1 tbsp.
- Cumin powder 1 tsp.
- Green chili 1 tsp.
- Turmeric 1 tsp.
- Frozen black beans 2 oz.
- Brazil nuts 2 oz.
- Tomato sauce 1 oz.
- Salt and fresh pepper to taste

Preparation Method

1. Heat in a large skillet pan; add ghee and onions on medium heat. Cook about 10 minutes. Add garlic and ginger, cook for another 2 minutes.
2. Add lamb to the pan and brown. Season with salt, pepper, cumin, coriander, green chili, turmeric and mix well.
3. Add coconut milk, brazil nuts, tomato sauce and water. Reduce heat to simmer about 20 minutes. Add frozen peas and simmer for an additional 15 minutes or until desired taste comes.

Nutritional Information

- Preparation Time: 35 minutes
- Total servings: 4
- Calories: 380.3 (per serving)
- Fat: 32.6g
- Protein: 17.2g
- Carbs: 8g

Recipe 74: Winter Vegetable Stew

Ingredients

- Winter vegetable mix 1 lb.
- Ghee 2 tbsp.
- Garlic powder 1 tsp.
- Ginger powder 1 tsp.
- Tomato puree 1.5 oz.
- All spice 1 ½ tbsp.
- Paprika 1 ½ tsp.
- Salt to taste
- Diced tomatoes 7 oz.
- Coconut milk 1 cup
- Walnut paste 1 tbsp.
- Coriander 1 ½ tbsp.

Topping:

- Grated mascarpone cheese

Preparation Method

1. At first, mix chopped winter vegetables into bite sized pieces and season with salt, pepper and garlic, ginger and mix well.
2. Add canned diced tomatoes and tomato paste, mix well again then add coconut milk, walnut paste and mix well.
3. Cook for 35 minutes on medium heat. Before serving, add ghee, grated mascarpone and enjoy extra flavor taste.

Nutritional Information

- Preparation Time: 40 minutes
- Serving per Recipe: 5
- Calories: 566.8 (per serving)
- Fat: 46.6g
- Protein: 22.2g
- Carbs: 6.3g

Recipe 75: Sesame Cabbage Biscuits

Ingredients

- Almond flour 1 ½ cup
- Cabbage 1.5 lb.
- Cheddar cheese 5 oz.
- Mascarpone cheese 4 oz.
- Ghee 2 oz.
- Large eggs 2
- Salt to taste
- Garlic powder 1 tsp.
- Baking soda ½ tsp.
- Toasted sesame seeds2 tbsp.

Preparation Method

1. At first, preheat your oven to 375F, blend cabbage until it is finely chopped.
2. In a large bowl, mix almond flour, salt, peppers, garlic powder, baking soda. Mix it well, add eggs and ghee. Mix until a dough forms.
3. Add your cabbage to the mixture. Combine everything with your hands. Grate cheddar and mascarpone to the dough. Mix everything with the hands until the cheese is evenly distributed.
4. Place your non-stick skillet on a cookie sheet, so that they do not stick as they boil. Form pies from the dough and sprinkle toasted sesame seeds. Bake like biscuits for 15 minutes or until they begin to flatten.
5. Turn it and continue baking for about 5 minutes then, turn your oven to roast and brew the biscuits for 3 minutes. Let it cool for 2 minutes before you enjoy the taste.

Nutritional Information

- Preparation Time: 30 minutes
- Total servings: 12
- Calories: 189 (per serving)
- Fat: 17.8g
- Protein: 7g
- Carbs: 3.3g

Recipe 76: Heavy Banana Bombs

Ingredients

- Ghee 4 oz.
- Heavy whipped cream 4 oz.
- Fresh cheese 4 oz.
- Berry extract 1 tsp.
- Stevia 10 drops
- Banana protein powder 1 oz.

Preparation Method

- At first, mix ghee, heavy cream and fresh cheese. Using a mixer, mix all the ingredients together or place in microwave oven for 30 seconds to 1 minute to soften them.
- Add berry extract and liquid stevia to the mixture and mix with a spoon.
- Distribute the mixture into a silicone tray and freeze for 3 hours.

Nutritional Information

- Preparation Time: 182 minutes
- Total servings: 10
- Calories: 186 (per serving)
- Fat: 18g
- Protein: 7.9g
- Carbs: 1g

Recipe 77: Crunchy Flax Biscuits

Ingredients

- Flax flour 1 ½ cup
- Ghee 2 oz.
- Salt to taste
- Baking soda ½ tsp.
- Cayenne pepper ¼ tsp.
- Ginger powder 1 tsp.
- Thyme 2 tbsp.

Preparation Method

1. At first, preheat oven to 325F. Place a cookie sheet with parchment paper.
2. In a medium bowl, mix flax flour, pepper, salt and baking powder.
3. Add dill, cayenne, ginger and stir until uniformly combined. Put the ghee into the cracker mixture with a fork until the dough forms a ball.
4. Transfer the dough to the prepared cookie sheet and spread the dough thinly until it is about 1 mm thick. Make sure the thickness is the same, so that the biscuits evenly bake.
5. Place the pan in the pre-heated oven then sprinkle thyme over it and bake for 15 minutes to light golden brown color. After baking, remove from the oven and cut into biscuits of the desired size.

Nutritional Information

- Preparation Time: 25 minutes
- Total servings: 6
- Calories:211 (per serving)
- Fat: 19.2g
- Protein: 5.4g
- Carbs: 2.8g

Recipe 78: Durian Mug Cake

Ingredients

- Durian 0.7 oz.
- Almond flour 2 tbsp.
- Chia flour 1 tbsp.
- Baking soda ⅛ tsp.
- Swerve 1 tbsp.
- Egg 1
- Fruit extracts ½ tsp.
- Ghee 1 tbsp.
- Whipped cream 2 tbsp.

Preparation Method

1. At first, place all the dry ingredients in a mug and combine well. Top with chopped durian.
2. Place mug in microwave on high for 90 seconds. Before serving add whipping cream and enjoy the taste.

Nutritional Information

- Preparation Time: 3 minutes
- Total servings: 1
- Calories: 349 (per serving)
- Fat: 24.9g
- Protein: 11.8g
- Carbs: 4.7g

Recipe 79: Energy Peanut Bars

Ingredients

- Coconut butter 1 cup
- Pumpkin purees 1 cup
- Ground cinnamon 1 tbsp.
- Peanuts 1 oz.
- Peanut butter 3 oz.
- Protein powder 2 oz.
- Ghee 2 tbsp.

Preparation Method

1. Hold aside 8x8 inch square baking tray with aluminum foil. In the large bowl, add melted coconut butter, peanut butter, pumpkin puree, spices, protein powder and mix well.
2. Add ghee and combine well without lumps. Pour the mixture into the already prepared pan and spread evenly then sprinkle chopped peanuts.
3. Cover with wax paper and evenly put into the pan. Remove wax paper and place the mixture in the refrigerator for 3 hours.
4. Use a sharp knife to cut into 25 equal squares and enjoy the delicious taste.

Nutritional Information

- Preparation Time: 15 minutes
- Total servings: 25
- Calories: 177 (per serving)
- Fat: 15.9g
- Protein: 7.7g
- Carbs: 2.6g

Recipe 80: Protein Flax Bars

Ingredients

- Flax ½ cup
- Ghee 2 oz.
- Maple syrup 1 oz.
- Cinnamon powder 1 tsp.
- Pinch of salt
- Cashew nuts 2 oz.
- Cashew butter 1 oz.
- Protein powder 2 oz.
- Shredded coconut 1 tbsp.

Preparation Method

1. At first, combine flax and melted ghee in a large bowl. Add cinnamon, salt and maple syrup, cashew butter, protein powder and mix well.
2. Add chopped cashews and mix everything evenly. Pour parchment paper into a casserole dish and spread the dough in a flat layer. Sprinkle crushed coconut and cinnamon up for beautiful crispy flavor.
3. Place them in a refrigerator and cool for 3 hours (night will give the best result). Cut into bars and enjoy the taste.

Nutritional Information

- Preparation Time:15 minutes
- Total servings: 8
- Calories: 199.5 (per serving)
- Fat: 21.7g
- Protein: 9.3g
- Carbs: 4.6g

Dessert Recipes

Recipe 81: Frozen Almond Banana Cups

Ingredients

- Dark chocolate 3.5 oz.
- Ghee 2 tbsp.
- Almond butter 4.5 oz.
- All spice 2 tsp.
- Erythritol 2 tbsp.
- Banana purees 3.5 oz.
- Protein powder 1 oz.
- Basil leaves 10 (frozen)
- Stevia 10 drops

Preparation Method

1. At first, melt dark chocolate and ghee by placing in microwave oven for 60 seconds and keep aside.
2. Fill 18 mini muffin cups with 2 teaspoons of chocolate and keep in fridge for at least 10 minutes.
3. In a small bowl, add protein powder, almond butter, ghee, erythritol and pumpkin spice mix and place in microwave oven for 60 seconds.
4. Now, add the banana puree and mix well until it combined. Remove the muffin cups from the fridge and add a 1 teaspoon of the banana and almond mixture into each cup.
5. Then add frozen basil leaves and place back in the fridge for 30 minutes and enjoy the taste.

Nutritional Information

- Preparation Time: 60 minutes
- Total servings: 18
- Calories: 131 (per serving)
- Fat: 12.1g
- Protein: 5g
- Carbs: 1.8g

Recipe 82: White Chia Cakes

Ingredients

- Chia meal 1 cup
- White chocolate 2 oz.
- Erythritol 4 tsp.
- Ghee 2 oz.
- Maple syrup 1 oz.
- Large eggs 2
- Baking soda 1 tsp.
- Salt ¼ tsp.
- Macadamia nut powder 1 oz.

Preparation Method

1. At first, preheat your oven to 350F. In small bowl, add erythritol, ghee, maple syrup, eggs and mix well.
2. In separate bowl, combine all chia meal, white chocolate, macadamia nut powder, baking soda and salt.
3. Mix bowl1 and bowl2 mixture using hand mixer then place batter into a 10x8 baking pan and bake for 20 minutes.
4. Let brownies cakes cool and slice it into 8 equal parts and enjoy eating while drinking coffee or tea.

Nutritional Information

- Preparation Time: 30 minutes
- Total servings: 8
- Calories: 278 (per serving)
- Fat: 22.2g
- Protein: 8.7g
- Carbs: 4.7g

Recipe 83: Fruit Nut Ice Cream

Ingredients

- Heavy cream 8 oz.
- Erythritol 2 oz.
- Cranberries 2 oz.
- Pineapple 1 oz.
- Avocado 1 oz.
- Protein powder 2 oz.
- Large egg yolks 3
- Nuts 12 tbsp.
- Vanillas extract 1 tsp.

Preparation Method

1. At first, place a pan over simmer and add heavy cream, erythritol, don't boil it just wait until erythritol is dissolved gently.
2. Meanwhile, add egg yolks in mixing bowl and beat using hand mixer until they've doubled in size.
3. Now, add hot cream mixture gently into the egg mixture and mix. Add vanilla extract, protein powder and mix well.
4. Place your bowl in the freezer for 2 hours minimum, don't forget stir occasionally.
5. Meanwhile, put cranberries, avocado, pineapple in a mixer (it should be little chunky). When the ice cream looks bit thicker, it's right time to add the chunky fruit paste and mix gently, but don't over mix.
6. Sprinkle nuts and let this ice cream chill for another 4 hours or overnight before you taste it.

Nutritional Information

- Preparation Time: 6.5 hours
- Total servings: 5
- Calories: 221 (per serving)
- Fat: 18.9g
- Protein: 8.9g
- Carbs: 2.8g

Recipe 84: Cranberry Frost Cups

Ingredients

Cake:
- Large eggs 6
- Cream cheese 3 oz.
- Cream of tartar 2 tsp.
- Erythritol 2 oz.
- Cranberries 6 pieces

Frosting:
- Cream cheese 1 lb.
- Ghee 1 oz.
- Erythritol mix 1 oz.
- Cranberries extract 1 tsp.
- Lemon juice 1 tbsp.

Preparation Method

1. At first, preheat your oven to 300 F. Spray 2 muffin tins with ghee then in a medium bowl, beat cream cheese, cranberries extract, sweetener and egg yolks until smooth.
2. In a separate bowl, whip the egg whites and cream of tartar with an electric mixer until stiff peaks form. Next, carefully fold the whipped egg whites into the yolk mixture.
3. Scoop about two tablespoons of the mixture into each muffin tin and gently press single cranberries into it then place in preheated oven and bake for 30 minutes or until golden brown.
4. Once done, remove the cake from the muffin tins and place on a cooling rack. While the cakes are cooling, combine all frosting ingredients together in a medium bowl.
5. Beat with an electric mixer until smooth. Transfer frosting to pastry bag with wide tip. Set aside 3 layers for each cake and then pipe frosting in between each layer of cake.

Nutritional Information

- Preparation Time: 45 minutes
- Total servings: 6
- Calories: 347 (per serving)
- Fat: 32.5g
- Protein: 10.5g
- Carbs: 4.1g

Recipe 85: Pecan Butter Ice Cream

Ingredients

- Coconut milk 1 ½ cup
- Heavy Cream ½ cup
- Butter ¼ cup
- Chopped pecans
- Liquid Stevia 25 drops
- Xanthan Gum ¼ tsp.

Preparation Method

1. In a pan over low heat, stir butter until golden color, add chopped or crushed pecans, heavy cream, stevia and stir together well
2. Add coconut milk, butter mixture, and xanthan gum to a container. Then use a whisk to mix everything together
3. Add mixture to your ice cream machine and run according to given manufacturers instructions. Serve and enjoy the taste

Nutritional Information

- Preparation Time: 10 minutes
- Serving per Recipe: 3
- Calories:319 (per serving)
- Protein: 0.7g
- Fat: 35.3g
- Carbohydrates: 1.3g

Recipe 86: Infused Avocado Sorbet

Ingredients

- Hass avocados 2
- Powdered erythritol 1 oz.
- 2 Lime juice
- 2 Lime zest
- Coconut milk 1 cup
- Liquid stevia 1 tbsp.
- Chopped cilantro 1 tbsp.

Preparation Method

1. Slice the avocados and remove pits from it and make 5 vertical slices using a knife
2. Add lime juice on top of all avocado slices and place in freezer for 2 hours
3. On the other hand, heat coconut milk and add lime zest, stir it for 2-3 minutes or until it looks thick
4. Shift to container and place in freezer for 10 minutes
5. Chop cilantro and take avocado from the freezer and make a paste by using a food processor (chunky consistency)
6. Pout coconut milk mixture, powdered erythritol and liquid stevia. Mix well until smooth or desired consistency (2-3 minutes)
7. Serve immediately or can store in freezer

Nutritional Information

- Preparation Time: 145 minutes
- Serving per Recipe: 4
- Calories: 180 (per serving)
- Protein: 2g
- Fat: 16g
- Carbohydrates: 3.5g

Recipe 87: Keto Coffee Cake

Ingredients

Base:

- Eggs 6
- Cream cheese ½ cup
- Erythritol 2 oz.
- Liquid stevia 1 oz.
- Optional: protein powder 1 oz.
- Vanilla extract 2 tsp.
- Cream of tartar 1 oz.

Filling:

- Almond flour 1 cup
- Cinnamon 1 tsp.
- Butter 4 oz.
- Maple syrup 1 oz.
- Erythritol 1 oz.

Preparation Method

1. Preheat the oven to 325F. In large bowl, add egg, erythritol and liquid stevia and mix well using hand mixer
2. Add cream cheese, protein powder and mix well until a thick batter forms
3. Mix egg into the tartar cream and pour the batter into a round cake pan
4. Mix together all filling ingredients and make dough and take half and rip off the little pieces on top the cake and push down in cake batter
5. Bake for 20 minutes and top with cinnamon filling and bake for another 20 minutes until a toothpick comes out clean
6. Cool it for 20 minutes and slice into 8 pieces and enjoy the taste

Nutritional Information

- Preparation Time: 70 minutes
- Serving per Recipe: 8
- Calories: 257 (per serving)
- Protein: 12.8g
- Fat: 26.7g
- Carbohydrates: 3.8g

Recipe 88: Cream Pots

Ingredients
- Heavy cream 1 cup
- Powdered erythritol 1 oz.
- Liquid stevia 1 tsp.
- Salt (as needed)
- Egg yolks 4
- Water ¼ cup
- Maple syrup 1 tbsp.
- Vanilla extract 1 tsp.
- Maple extract 1 tsp.

Preparation Method
1. Preheat the oven to 300F and whisk egg yolks finely
2. Mix water with erythritol in small pan and start boiling on low heat. After 1 minute, add maple syrup and keep aside
3. In another medium bowl, mix cream, stevia, salt, extracts and start boiling on low heat and add water syrup (first bowl) into batter and add whisk egg yolk
4. Mix well until it looks smooth and soft
5. Add to small cups and keep in oven for 10-15 minutes or until it looks like the pudding texture and sprinkle with cinnamon for flavor and enjoy the taste

Nutritional Information
- Preparation Time: 20 minutes
- Serving per Recipe: 4
- Calories: 359 (per serving)
- Protein: 2.8g
- Fat: 34.9g
- Carbohydrates: 3g

Recipe 89: Chocolate Pie

Ingredients

Crust:

- Almond flour 1 cup
- Baking powder ½ tsp.
- Salt pinch
- Granulated stevia/erythritol blend 3 oz.
- Butter 2 oz.
- Egg 1
- Vanilla extract 1 tsp.
- Butter (for greasing the pan) 1 tsp.

Filling:

- Cream cheese 1 lb.
- Sour cream 4 tbsp.
- Butter 4 tbsp.
- Vanilla extract 1 tbsp.
- Granulated stevia/erythritol blend ½ cup
- Cocoa powder ½ cup
- Whipping cream 1 cup
- Granulated stevia/erythritol blend, for whipped cream 2 tsp.
- Vanilla extract, for whipped cream 1 tsp.

Preparation Method

1. Preheat oven to 375 F. Generously butter a 9" pie pan with butter. In a medium mixing bowl, combine almond flour, baking powder, salt and 1/3 cup stevia/erythritol blend. Using a whisk, blend the dry ingredients together
2. Add butter to dry ingredients. Using a pastry blender, whisk or a fork, cut the butter into dry ingredients until the mixture forms into coarse crumbs
3. Add egg and vanilla extract and stir until the dough forms into a ball. Transfer the dough to the prepared pan and spread out the dough using your fingers until it evenly covers the bottom and sides of the pan.
4. Wetting your hands with cold water can help prevent the dough from sticking to your fingers. Flute edges if desired. Using a fork, poke holes in the bottom and sides of crust to prevent bubbles from forming as it bakes
5. Place crust in the oven and bake for 11 minutes. Remove crust from the oven and loosely cover edges with foil. Return it to oven for 5 to 8 more minutes or until the bottom of the crust is golden brown. Allow the crust to cool completely before filling
6. To prepare the filling, place cream cheese, sour cream, butter, vanilla extract, ½ cup stevia/erythritol blend and cocoa powder in a medium bowl
7. Using a mixer on low speed, blend ingredients to combine, then increase to high speed and beat until fluffy. Place the whipping cream in a separate small bowl. Using clean mixer beaters
8. Add the 2 teaspoons sweetener and vanilla extract and beat until stiff peaks form. Gently fold 1/3 of the whipped cream mixture into the cream cheese mixture to lighten. Add remaining whipped cream mixture and fold it in gently.
9. The idea is to blend the two mixtures together without breaking the bubbles in the cream. Scoop the filling into the crust and smooth the top with a spoon

10. Cover and refrigerate your keto chocolate silk pie for at least 3 hours before serving

Nutritional Information

- Preparation Time: 210 minutes
- Serving per Recipe: 10
- Calories:447 (per serving)
- Protein: 5.9g
- Fat: 41.9g
- Carbohydrates: 7.2g

Recipe 90: Creme Cookie Ice

Ingredients

Cookie Crumbs:
- Almond flour 4 oz.
- Cocoa powder 1 oz.
- Baking soda pinch
- Erythritol 2 oz.
- Vanilla extract pinch
- Coconut oil 1 ½ tbsp.
- Egg 1
- Pinch of salt

Ice Cream:
- 2 1/2 cups whipping cream
- Vanilla extract 1 tbsp.
- Erythritol ½ cup
- Almond milk ½ cup

Preparation Method

1. Preheat oven to 300F. Line 9 inch circular cake pan with parchment paper and spray with oil of choice. Put almond flour, cocoa powder, baking soda, erythritol, and salt into a medium bowl and then whisk until smooth
2. Add the vanilla extract and coconut oil and mix until batter forms into fine crumbs. Add the egg and blend until cookie batter begins to stick together and form a ball
3. Transfer the batter into prepared cake pan and press out batter thinly with your fingers until it evenly covers the bottom of the pan. Place pan in preheated oven and bake for 20 minutes or until center of cookie bounces back when pressed
4. When finished baking, remove pan from oven and let cool. Once the cookie has cooled, break the cookie into small crumbles. In a large bowl, blend the whipping cream with an electric mixer until stiff peaks form
5. Add vanilla extract and erythritol, and whip until thoroughly combined.
6. Pour in almond milk and blend mixture until it re-thickens. Transfer cream mixture to ice cream maker and churn until ice cream begins to hold its shape
7. Gradually pour the cookie crumbles in while the ice cream maker is churning to evenly mix the crumbles into the ice cream. Once all of the cookie crumbles are incorporated, transfer the ice cream into a ½ gallon freezer-safe container and freeze for at least 2 hours before serving

Nutritional Information

- Preparation Time: 140 minutes
- Serving per Recipe: 10
- Calories:194 (per serving)
- Protein: 3.5g
- Fat: 18.3g
- Carbohydrates: 4.5g

Recipe 91: Cranberry Ice Cream

Ingredients

- Heavy cream 8 oz.
- Erythritol 2 oz.
- Cranberries 6 oz.
- Banana protein powder 2 oz.
- Large egg yolks 3
- Pineapples extract 1/2 tsp.
- Nuts 12 tbsp.

Preparation Method

1. At first, place a pan over simmer and add heavy cream, erythritol, don't boil it just wait until erythritol is dissolved gently.
2. Meanwhile, add egg yolks in mixing bowl and beat using hand mixer until they've doubled in size.
3. Now, add hot cream mixture gently into the egg mixture and mix. Add pineapples extract, banana protein powder and mix well.
4. Place your bowl in the freezer for 2 hours minimum, don't forget stir occasionally.
5. Meanwhile, put cranberries in a mixer (it should be little chunky). When the ice cream looks bit thicker, it's right time to add the chunky cranberries and mix gently, but don't over mix.
6. Sprinkle nuts and let this ice cream chill for another 4 hours or overnight before you taste it.

Nutritional Information

- Preparation Time: 6.5 hours
- Total servings: 5
- Calories: 221 (per serving)
- Fat: 17.2g
- Protein: 8.9g
- Carbs: 2.5g

Recipe 92: Cucunach Smoothie

Ingredients

- Spinach 10 oz.
- Cucumber ½
- Ice cubes 7
- Coconut milk 1 cup
- Liquid stevia 12 drops
- Xanthan gum pinch
- Coconut oil 4 tsp.

Preparation Method

1. In blender, place all ingredients and blend on medium speed or until smooth
2. Pour into serving glass and enjoy the taste

Nutritional Information

- Preparation Time: 5 minutes
- Serving per Recipe: 1
- Calories:335 (per serving)
- Protein: 3g
- Fat: 33g
- Carbohydrates: 7g

Recipe 93: Cara Milk Smoothie

Ingredients

- Ice cubes 7
- Coconut milk 1 cup
- Peanut butter 1 oz.
- Caramel 2 tbsp.
- Coconut oil 1 tbsp.

Preparation Method

1. In blender, place all ingredients and blend on medium speed or until smooth
2. Pour into serving glass and enjoy the taste

Nutritional Information

- Preparation Time: 5 minutes
- Serving per Recipe: 1
- Calories:336 (per serving)
- Protein: 7g
- Fat: 35g
- Carbohydrates: 6g

Recipe 94: Coco Seed Smoothie

Ingredients

- Ice cubes 7
- Coconut milk 1 cup
- Sour cream ¼ cup
- Flaxseed meal 1 oz.
- Coconut oil 1 tbsp.
- Liquid stevia 20 drops
- Mango extract 1 tsp.
- Blueberry extract ½ tsp.
- Banana extract pinch

Preparation Method

1. In blender, place all ingredients and blend on medium speed or until smooth
2. Pour into serving glass and enjoy the taste

Nutritional Information

- Preparation Time: 5 minutes
- Serving per Recipe: 1
- Calories:352 (per serving)
- Protein: 5g
- Fat: 31g
- Carbohydrates: 3g

Recipe 95: Ripe Avocado Smoothie

Ingredients

- Ripe avocado 1
- Frozen raspberries 4 oz.
- Water 2 cups
- Lemon juice 1 oz.
- Stevia 20 drops

Preparation Method

1. In blender, place all ingredients and blend on medium speed or until smooth
2. Pour into serving glass and enjoy the taste

Nutritional Information

- Preparation Time:2 minutes
- Serving per Recipe: 2
- Calories: 227 (per serving)
- Protein:2.5 g
- Fat: 20g
- Carbohydrates: 4g

Recipe 96: Butter Rhubarb Smoothie

Ingredients

- Rhubarb stalks 1 oz.
- Strawberries 2 oz.
- Almond butter 1 oz.
- Egg 1
- Almond milk ½ cup
- Cream 1 oz.
- Ginger root powder pinch
- Vanilla extract 1 tsp.
- Stevia 6 drops

Preparation Method

1. In blender, place all ingredients and blend on medium speed or until smooth
2. Pour into serving glass and enjoy the taste

Nutritional Information

- Preparation Time: 5 minutes
- Serving per Recipe: 1
- Calories: 392 (per serving)
- Protein: 14.2g
- Fat: 31.8g
- Carbohydrates: 8.6g

Recipe 97: Chia Banana Smoothie

Ingredients

- Flax seed meal 1 oz.
- Chia seeds 1 tbsp.
- Coconut milk 1 ½ cup
- Liquid stevia 10 drops
- Blueberries 3 oz.
- Banana extract 1 tsp.
- Ice cubes 7

Preparation Method

1. Blend the coconut milk with 7 ice cubes, banana extract, stevia
2. Add blueberries, flax meal, chia seed and blend until ingredients are fully incorporated
3. Measure out into serving and enjoy the taste

Nutritional Information

- Preparation Time: 10 minutes
- Serving per Recipe: 2
- Calories: 264 (per serving)
- Protein: 4g
- Fat: 25g
- Carbohydrates: 3g

Recipe 98: Cream Coco Smoothie

Ingredients

- Blackberries 3 oz.
- Cream cheese 2 oz.
- Coconut milk ½ cup
- Water ½ cup
- Extra virgin coconut oil 1 tbsp.
- Vanilla extract 1 tsp.

Preparation Method

1. In blender, place all ingredients and blend on medium speed or until smooth
2. Pour into serving glass and enjoy the taste

Nutritional Information

- Preparation Time: 5 minutes
- Serving per Recipe: 1
- Calories: 515 (per serving)
- Protein: 6.4g
- Fat: 53g
- Carbohydrates: 6.7g

Recipe 99: Heavy Keto Smoothie

Ingredients

- Heavy whipping cream ¼ cup
- Almond milk ½ cup
- Strawberries 3 oz.
- Extra virgin coconut oil 1 tbsp.
- Pineapple extract 1 tsp.

Preparation Method

1. In blender, place all ingredients and blend on medium speed or until smooth
2. Pour into serving glass and enjoy the taste

Nutritional Information

- Preparation Time: 5 minutes
- Serving per Recipe: 1
- Calories: 275 (per serving)
- Protein: 2.5g
- Fat:27.4 g
- Carbohydrates: 6.4g

Recipe 100: Mexican Cream Smoothie

Ingredients

- Coconut cream (3 oz.)
- Extra virgin coconut oil 1 oz.
- Ground chia seeds 2 tsp.
- Cocoa powder 2 tsp.
- Vanilla extract 1 tsp.
- Cinnamon powder pinch
- Cayenne powder pinch
- Water 1 cup
- Ice cubes 5

Preparation Method

1. In blender, place all ingredients and blend on medium speed or until smooth
2. Pour into serving glass and enjoy the taste

Nutritional Information

- Preparation Time: 5 minutes
- Serving per Recipe: 1
- Calories: 503 (per serving)
- Protein: 6g
- Fat: 43.1g
- Carbohydrates: 6.2g

Bonus Recipe 101: Keto Seasoned Coffee

Ingredients

- Coffee 1 cup (240 ml)
- Unsalted butter 1 tbsp.
- Coconut oil 1 tbsp.
- Heavy cream 1 tbsp.
- Seasonings to taste

Preparation Method

- At first, make 1 cup of coffee and put in serving glass
- Now, add butter, after it ooze then coconut oil, heavy cream and mix well
- It gives creaminess and extra flavor to the coffee
- If desired, add your favorite seasonings like cinnamon, nutmeg, or allspice with a splash of liquid stevia
- Mix it all together very well using a hand blender and enjoy the taste

Nutritional Information

- Preparation Time: 5 minutes
- Serving per Recipe: 1
- Calories: 273
- Protein: 0g
- Fat: 30g
- Carbohydrates: 1g

Conversion Table

Cups, Tablespoons and Teaspoons Details

- 1 tablespoon = 15 ml
- 1 teaspoon = 5 ml
- 1 cup = 16 tablespoons = 48 teaspoons = 240 ml
- 3/4 cup = 12 tablespoons = 36 teaspoons = 180 ml
- 2/3 cup = 11 tablespoons = 32 teaspoons = 160 ml
- 1/2 cup = 8 tablespoons = 24 teaspoons = 120 ml
- 1/3 cup = 5 tablespoons = 16 teaspoons = 80 ml
- 1/4 cup = 4 tablespoons = 12 teaspoons = 60 ml

Cup to Fluid Ounces (cup to fl. oz)

- 1 tablespoon = 0.5 fl oz
- 1 fl oz = 2 tablespoons = 6 teaspoons
- 1 cup = 8 fl oz
- 3/4 cup = 6 fl oz
- 2/3 cup = 5 fl oz
- 1/2 cup = 4 fl oz
- 1/3 cup = 3 fl oz
- 1/4 cup = 2 fl oz

Ounces to Grams

- 1 ounce = 28 grams
- 2 ounces = 55 grams
- 3 ounces = 85 grams
- 3.5 ounces = 100 grams
- 4 ounces = 115 grams
- 5 ounces = 140 grams
- 6 ounces = 170 grams
- 8 ounces = 225 grams
- 10 ounces = 285 grams
- 12 ounces = 340 grams
- 16 ounces = 1 pound = 455 grams

Pounds to Grams and Kilograms

- 1/4 pound = 115 grams
- 1/2 pound = 225 grams
- 3/4 pound = 340 grams
- 1 pound = 455 grams
- 1.25 pounds = 567 grams
- 1.5 pounds = 680 grams
- 2 pounds = 908 grams
- 2.5 pounds = 1.15 kilograms
- 3 pounds = 1.35 kilograms

Flour (cup to grams)
- 1 cup flour = 140 grams
- 3/4 cup flour = 105 grams
- 2/3 cup flour = 93 grams
- 1/2 cup flour = 70 grams
- 1/3 cup flour = 47 grams
- 1/4 cup flour = 35 grams
- 1 tablespoon flour = 9 grams

Butter (cup, stick, pound, ounce, gram)
- 1 pound butter = 455 grams
- 1 cup butter = 2 sticks = 8 ounces = 230 grams
- 1 stick butter = 4 ounces = 115 grams
- 14 tablespoons butter = 200 grams = 7 ounces
- 12 tablespoons butter = 170 grams = 6 ounces
- 10 tablespoons butter = 140 grams = 5 ounces
- 9 tablespoons butter = 125 grams = 4.5 ounces
- 7 tablespoons butter = 100 grams = 3.5 ounces
- 6 tablespoons butter = 85 grams = 3 ounces
- 5 tablespoons butter = 70 grams = 2.5 ounces
- 3 tablespoons butter = 40 grams = 1.5 ounces
- 1 tablespoon butter = 15 grams = 0.5 ounces

Fahrenheit (°F) to Celcius (°C) to Gas
- 250°F = 120°C = gas mark 1/2
- 275°F = 135°C = gas mark 1
- 300°F = 150°C = gas mark 2
- 325°F = 160°C = gas mark 3
- 350°F = 175°C = gas mark 4
- 375°F = 190°C = gas mark 5
- 400°F = 200°C = gas mark 6
- 425°F = 220°C = gas mark 7
- 450°F = 230°C = gas mark 8
- 475°F = 245°C = gas mark 9
- 500°F = 260°C = gas mark 10

Milk (cups to grams)
- 1 cup milk = 240 grams
- 3/4 cup milk = 180 grams
- 2/3 cup milk = 160 grams
- 1/2 cup milk = 120 grams
- 1/3 cup milk = 80 grams
- 1/4 cup milk = 60 grams
- 1 tablespoon milk = 15 grams

Heavy Cream (cups to grams)
- 1 cup heavy cream = 240 grams

- 3/4 cup heavy cream = 180 grams
- 2/3 cup heavy cream = 160 grams
- 1/2 cup heavy cream = 120 grams
- 1/3 cup heavy cream = 80 grams
- 1/4 cup heavy cream = 60 grams
- 1 tablespoon heavy cream = 15 grams

Cinnamon/Ginger/Allspice (ground)

- 1 tablespoon ground cinnamon (or ginger or allspice) = 9 grams
- 1 teaspoon ground cinnamon = 3 grams
- 3/4 teaspoon ground cinnamon = 2 grams
- 1/2 teaspoon ground cinnamon = 2 grams
- 1/4 teaspoon ground cinnamon = 1 gram

CONCLUSION

KETOGENIC DIET is the key to your success to achieve your dream in the right way but in short time. This book offers high energizing information, including nutritional recipes with fully packed fat, protein, crabs, vitamins, minerals, antioxidants and phytochemicals to the body. Fat burning is vastly elevated even as insulin, this creates best situations in which fat loss can arise, without starvation. Overall benefits that you are going to get from ketogenic diet are:

- Rapid weight loss
- Type 2 diabetes reversed
- Increased mental focus
- Improved physical endurance
- Metabolic syndrome
- Epilepsy controlling
- Decreasing cancers
- Controlled blood pressure
- Less stomach problems
- Acne control
- Decreasing heartburn
- Decreasing migraine attacks
- Decreasing sugar cravings
- Reverse PCOS

Are you wondering for the right guide to start Keto Diet?
Then this book will guide you in the right way to achieve your dream to lose weight and strengthen your body system by boosting energy and vitality. For a few humans, it's far very smooth to drop a sizable amount of weight on the ketogenic diet in less time. Normally a weight reduction stabilizes in the regular weight variety, so long as you eat while hungry and don't starve yourself.

In this book, you are going to learn:
- Step by step guide to start the ketogenic diet in the right way
- User friendly grocery shopping list for every week
- Yummy recipes of Breakfast, Lunch, Dinner, Salad, Soup, Snack and Smoothies
- Each recipe will have nutritional information like calories, fat, protein and carbs details
- And many more tips and tricks inside!

Overall
The Ketogenic Diet isn't always a cure enthusiastic about each sick in the world, however, it could pretty much come up with what you need if you are trying to lose weight effectively without a whole lot exercise, get your body's metabolism in the form to be rid of those bad cardiovascular symptoms and dramatically carry up your energy levels day by day.

Don't think about tomorrow, just start your Ketogenic journey today to achieve your dream in short time. Don't forget to take measurements and photos before you start your diet; this is the best way to monitor your progress and remember this is not just for weight loss, this is for achieving better health throughout your life. Once again thank you for downloading our book, and we hope you will achieve your dream weight and health.

ABOUT THE AUTHOR

Hello! I'm Tanya Baker, one of the passionate follower of Ketogenic diet. I live in the USA. I have been espousing ketogenic diet since 23 years old. Frankly Ketogenic is not a diet; it's a lifestyle. Basically, I hate being overweight and having fatty body; we should be slimmer and more active in out daily life. While following this way of lifestyle, you are going to improve your health and beauty with dramatic weight loss in short time. I sincerely recommend you to follow a ketogenic diet and explore yourself lots of benefits.

HOW I FEEL

I feel wonderful to be a follower of ketogenic diet and one good thing is I choose and make my own ketogenic recipes without any deficiency of fat, protein and crabs. Due to busy daily work tensions, lot of people are not able to create or make there own recipes, so I want to share and help you to prepare my recipes for healthy file.

-- [Tanya Baker]

Made in the USA
Middletown, DE
25 March 2018